4

Life

SECOND EDITION

NATIONAL GEOGRAPHIC
LEARNING

HELEN STEPHENSON
DAVID BOHLKE

Australia · Brazil · Mexico · Singapore · United Kingdom · United States

NATIONAL GEOGRAPHIC
LEARNING

Life 4 Workbook, Second Edition
Helen Stephenson, David Bohlke

Vice President, Editorial Director:
John McHugh

Publisher: Andrew Robinson

Senior Development Editor: Derek Mackrell

Editorial Assistant: Dawne Law

Director of Global Marketing: Ian Martin

Senior Product Marketing Manager:
Caitlin Thomas

Media Researcher: Rebecca Ray,
Leila Hishmeh

Senior IP Analyst: Alexandra Ricciardi

IP Project Manager: Carissa Poweleit

Senior Director, Production:
Michael Burggren

Production Manager: Daisy Sosa

Content Project Manager: Beth McNally

Manufacturing Planner:
Mary Beth Hennebury

Art Director: Brenda Carmichael

Cover Design: Lisa Trager

Text Design: emc design ltd.

Compositor: DoubleInk Publishing Services

For product information and technology assistance, contact us at
Cengage Learning Customer & Sales Support, cengage.com/contact

For permission to use material from this text or product,
submit all requests online at **cengage.com/permissions**
Further permissions questions can be emailed to
permissionrequest@cengage.com

ISBN: 978-1-337-90800-9

National Geographic Learning
20 Channel Center Street
Boston, MA 02210
USA

National Geographic Learning, a Cengage Learning Company, has a mission to bring the world to the classroom and the classroom to life. With our English language programs, students learn about their world by experiencing it. Through our partnerships with National Geographic and TED Talks, they develop the language and skills they need to be successful global citizens and leaders.

Locate your local office at **international.cengage.com/region**

Visit National Geographic Learning online at **NGL.Cengage.com/ELT**
Visit our corporate website at **www.cengage.com**

Credits
Although every effort has been made to contact copyright holders before publication, this has not always been possible. If notified, the publisher will undertake to rectify any errors or omissions at the earliest opportunity.

Text: p8: adapted from: 'Getting to The Heart of The Appeal of Videogames', by Andrew Przybylski, http://www.psychologicalscience.org/news/releases/getting-to-the-heart-of-the-appeal-of-videogames.html#.WCRjhzW53uc; p12: source: 'Barcelona Street Life', http://www.natgeoeducationvideo.com/film/455/barcelona-street-life; p16: adapted from: 'Life in a Day: Around the world in 80,000 clips', http://www.guardian.co.uk/film/2011/jun/07/life-in-a-day-macdonald?INTCMP=SRCH, and adapted from: 'Life in a Day', www.nationalgeographic.com; p18: source: 'Portrait of the artist: Ravi Shankar, musician', by Laura Barnett, June 06, 2011, http://www.guardian.co.uk/culture/2011/jun/06/ravi-shankar-musician; p20: source: http://ngm.nationalgeographic.com/2007/03/bahamian-sharks/skerry-field-notes; p22: source: 'Hurricane Mitch', http://environment.nationalgeographic.com/environment/natural-disasters/hurricane-profile, and adapted from: 'Hurricane Mitch', http://environment.nationalgeographic.com/environment/photos/climate-change/#/climate-desert-honduras_13082_600x450.jpg and wikipedia; p24: source: 'Bottled water free town', www.bundyontap.com.au; p36: source: Boyd recalls a memorable meal he hand-picked with an Aborigine guide in the Australian outback', by Boyd Manson, www.nationalgeographic.com; p39: adapted from: 'Strategies for Success', http://www.nationalgeographic.com/pathways/index.html; p44: source: 'Queuing', by Keith Moore, September 07, 2015, http://www.bbc.com/news/magazine-34153628; http://www.dailymail.co.uk/sciencetech/article-3197487/Have-queuing-wrong-Lines-faster-person-served-study-finds.html; p46: source: 'Easter Island' http://blogs.ngm.com/blog_central/2010/11/easter-island-hats.html; p48: source: 'Crop Circles: Evidence of collusion between marsupials and extraterrestrials?', by patrickjkiger, August 04, 2011, http://tvblogs.nationalgeographic.com/2011/08/04/crop-circles-evidence-of-collusion-between-marsupials-and-extraterrestrials/; p49: source: 'Reacting to surprising news: yet', http://www.guardian.co.uk/environment/2011/oct/18/endangered-tuna-trade-quota?INTCMP=SRCH; p53: adapted from: 'Timbuktu', http://travel.nationalgeographic.com/travel/world-heritage/timbuktu/; p55: adapted from: 'An eco-village', http://naturalhomes.org/timeline/matavenero.htm, http://proof.nationalgeographic.com/2015/10/01/tired-of-the-bustle-of-modern-life-virtually-visit-this-eco-village; p56: source: 'Urban Visionary', by Keith Bellows, www.nationalgeographic.com; p58: source: 'I love my city', Keith's Amsterdam, August 19, 2011, http://intelligenttravel.nationalgeographic.com/2011/08/19/i-heart-my-city-keiths-amsterdam/; p60: http://travel.nationalgeographic.com/travel/traveler-magazine/one-on-one/a-master-storyteller/; p62: adapted from: 'Seen the movie? See the real place!', http://travel.nationalgeographic.com/travel/top-10/film-locations/; p70: source: 'Predictable passwords', by Catherine Zuckerman, http://ngm.nationalgeographic.com; p79: source: 'What can the body take?', National Geographic Magazine, October 2009; p80: source: 'Our brains are already "limitless"', by Marc Silver, 18 March 2011, http://blogs.ngm.com; p84: source: http://www.nationalgeographic.com/field/explorers/paula-kahumbu/; p86: 'Mobile technology and the art of the possible', by Ken Banks, http://video.nationalgeographic.com/video/news/ken-banks-es; p88: source: 'Words and time', by Jeremy Berlin, www.nationalgeographic.com; p94: 'A man of many talents', by Tuy Sereivathana, www.nationalgeographic.com/explorers/bios/tuy-sereivathana/; p96: source: 'Expert animals', by Virginia Morell, March 2008, www.nationalgeographic.com.

Cover: © Getty Images.

Photos: 4 © ventdusud/Shutterstock.com; 6 © bibikoff/iStockphoto; 8 Richard G. Bingham II/Alamy Stock Photo; 12 © Richard Nowitz/National Geographic Creative; 15 © AP Photo/Alan Welner/AP Images; 16 © grzym/Shutterstock.com; 18 Dinodia Photos/Alamy Stock Photo; 20 © Brian J. Skerry/National Geographic Creative; 22 © AP Photo/Gregory Bull/AP Images; 24 © Africa Studio/Shutterstock.com; 25 © Natali_ua/Shutterstock.com; 26 Stephen Barnes/Titanic/Alamy Stock Photo; 28–29 © John Stanmeyer/National Geographic Creative; 30 © Catherine Karnow/National Geographic Creative; 32–33 © Jacob Wackerhausen/iStockphoto; 33 © wavebreakmedia/Shutterstock.com; 34 © Robert Kneschke/Shutterstock.com; 36 Bill Bachman/Alamy Stock Photo; 37 (bl) Eric Ehrlich/Shutterstock.com; 39 © Patricia Hofmeester/Shutterstock.com; 40 © Pete McBride/National Geographic Creative; 41 Wavebreak Media/Alamy Stock Photo; 42 Scott Hortop Life/Alamy Stock Photo; 44 © Sunflowerey/Shutterstock.com; 46 © Alexander Chaikin/Shutterstock.com; 48 (tl) © canbedone/Shutterstock.com; 48 (tr) © Ruth Black/Shutterstock.com; 48 (bl) © Vishnevskiy Vasily/Shutterstock.com; 48 (br) © Julia Reschke/Shutterstock.com; 49 (l) © Alekcey/Shutterstock.com; 49 (r) © Ricardo De Mattos/iStockphoto; 50 © Shvaygert Ekaterina/Shutterstock.com; 52 © Hector Conesa/Shutterstock.com 53 © Sean Caffrey/Getty Images; 55 © Kevin Faingnaert; 58 © jan kranendonk/Shutterstock.com; 60 © Boyd Matson; 62 © Sourav and Joyeeta/Shutterstock.com; 63 © Stringer/Getty Images; 64 © Maridav/Shutterstock.com; 65 (br) Vietnam Stock Images/Shutterstock.com; 66 © Miguel Cabezón/Shutterstock.com; 68 (t) © Randy Olson/National Geographic Creative; 68 (b) © Joe Petersburger/National Geographic Creative; 69 (l) © Richard Nowitz/National Geographic Creative; 69 (m) © Daleen Loest/Shutterstock.com; 69 (tr) © Susanne Karlsson/Shutterstock.com; 69 (br) © homydesign/Shutterstock.com; 71 (br) Image Source / Alamy Stock Photo; 72 (tl) © Soyka/Shutterstock.com; 72 (tr) © Danicek/Shutterstock.com; 72 (bl) © Elena Schweitzer/Shutterstock.com; 72 (br) © Fatseyeva/Shutterstock.com; 73 © Anna Zielinska/iStockphoto; 74 (t) Ljupcho Jovkovski/Alamy Stock Photo; 74 (b) © StockPhotosArt/Shutterstock.com; 76 © kali9/iStockphoto; 77 (t) © Natalia Pushchina/Shutterstock.com; 77 (b) © bensliman hassan/Shutterstock.com; 80 © Cary Wolinsky/National Geographic Creative; 82 © Tatagatta/Shutterstock.com; 85 © Charlie Forgham-Bailey/eyevine/Redux; 86 © James Bedford/National Geographic Creative; 88 © Oliver Uberti/National Geographic Creative; 89 © Stockbyte/Getty Images; 92 (tl) © David Cheskin/PA Wire/AP Images; 92 (tr) © AP Photo/Elise Amendola/AP Images; 92 (m) Keystone Pictures USA/Alamy Stock Photo; 92 (bl) © Robert I.M. Campbell/National Geographic Creative; 92 (br) © AP Photo/Khalil Senosi/AP Images; 93 © Herbert G. Ponting/National Geographic Creative; 94 © Gosiek-B/iStockphoto; 96 © Robert Sisson/National Geographic Creative; 97 © Jennifer_Sharp/iStockphoto; 98 © Image Source/Getty Images.

Illustrations: 13, 47 (Pukao), 57, 71, 81, 85 Kevin Hopgood/Kevin Hopgood Illustration; 22 Oxford Designers & Illustrators; 47 (globe), 53, 56, 72 David Russell; 51, 66, 99 (3, 4, 5, 7) Lumina Datamatics; 75, 99 (1, 2, 6) Gary Wing; 79, 95 Matthew Hams.

Printed at CLDPC, USA, 02-23

Contents

Unit 1 Culture and identity

1a National identity

Listening identity

1 ▶ 01 Listen to an excerpt from a radio program on national identity. Answer these questions. Then listen and check your ideas.

1 What is the national sport of the United States?

| (baseball) | basketball | cricket | soccer |

2 In what state does the famous highway Route 66 end?

| (California) | Florida | Hawaii | New York |

2 ▶ 01 Listen to the excerpt again. Number the things in the order that they are mentioned (1–5).

e a movies
d b road trips
a c slang
c d fast food
b e baseball

3 ▶ 01 Complete the sentences with the simple present or present continuous form of the verbs. Then listen again and check.

1 As usual on Friday's show, we *are asking* (ask) you at home a question.

2 I *'m eating* (eat) a cheeseburger and French fries right now!"

3 Now you *'re making* (make) me hungry.

4 That *seems* (seem) like a bad idea to me.

5 I'm Brazilian, but I *'m living* (live) in Los Angeles now.

6 I *love* (love) to use words like "cool," "awesome," and "chill."

7 We *go* (go) to a different place every year.

8 I *'m sitting* (sit) here looking at a gray studio wall.

Grammar simple present and present continuous

4 Complete the paragraph with the simple present or present continuous forms of the verbs in parentheses.

I'm from Daejon, South Korea, and I'm a college student. I'm studying in Vancouver at the moment. I [1] *have* (have) a scholarship to study here for one semester. I [2] *love* (love) my life here, and I [3] *'m making* (make) a lot of new friends from different parts of the world. My English [4] *is getting* (get) better and better. It's pretty easy to fit in here.

Most of the students in my classes are from Asia, Europe, and South America. Canada is a bilingual country, so most people [5] *speak* (speak) both English and French. Right now my French isn't very good, but I [6] *'m living* (learn) slowly. I [7] *study* (study) with a tutor three nights a week. My tutor says my pronunciation is good, but I [8] *don't believe* (not / believe) her.

Sometimes my friends and I [9] *play* (play) a game when we are out in the city. We try to identify other people from the same country as us. It [10] *sounds* (sound) easy, but it isn't. For example, my friend Luigi says that all Italians [11] *dress* (dress) in a similar way, but I [12] *don't agree* (not / agree) with him.

Grammar dynamic and stative verbs

5 Complete the sentences with the correct form of the verb in parentheses.

1 I _agree_ (agree) with everything you said to Martin.

2 I'm sorry you don't feel well. I _hope_ (hope) you get better soon.

3 _Do_ you _recognize_ (recognize) this boy in the photo?

4 I really _don't remember_ (not / remember) where I put my keys last night.

5 _Are_ you _thinking_ (think) about going to Italy again?

6 Which classes _are_ you _taking_ (take) this year?

7 That _seems_ (seem) like a lot to pay for a concert ticket.

8 This soup _don't taste_ (not / taste) right. Did you use salt or sugar?

9 We have some good news—Jenna _is expecting_ (expect) a baby.

6 Look at the example. Write sentences (affirmative or negative) that are true for you. Use the correct form of the verb.

1 believe in ghosts
   I believe in ghosts. / I don't believe in ghosts.

2 wear sandals today
   I'm wearing / I'm not wearing

3 remember my first day of school
   I remember / I don't remember

4 think about going to the library
   I'm taking / I'm not taking

5 need a day off
   I need / I don't need

6 feel great today
   I feel / I don't feel

7 prefer mornings to evenings
   I prefer / I don't prefer

8 get up late on weekends
   I get up / I don't get up

9 know how to speak Chinese
   I know / I don't know

10 understand the difference between dynamic and stative verbs
   I understand / I don't understand

7 Vocabulary extra common errors

Complete the sentences with the words. They all appear in the Reading text on page 10 of the Student's Book.

behavior	curious	everyday
in the case	opinion	predictions

1 Greg, what's your _opinion_ of this suggestion?

2 The teacher was pleased with the _behavior_ of her class on the school trip.

3 I don't like making _predictions_ about my exam results. It's bad luck.

4 I'm _curious_ about why you didn't finish the essay portion of the exam.

5 All the exams last one hour, but _in the case_ of English, the exam is 90 minutes.

6 We don't usually meet celebrities in _everyday_ life.

Word focus *love*

8 Match the two parts of the exchanges.

1 Brian is staying with us right now. _f_
2 I'm so surprised Jo and Pete have split up. _b_
3 Is your brother living in Paris now? _g_
4 My sister is studying to be a vet. _e_
5 You've invited a lot of people! _d_
6 What's this TV show about? _a_
7 Would you like some coffee? _h_
8 Would you like to go for a walk? _c_

a It's about a man who falls in love with his neighbor.
b I know. Pete said Jo was the love of his life.
c Sure. I'd love to!
d I know, but it's OK. I love cooking for my friends.
e Oh, I'd love to work with animals.
f Oh, please give him our love.
g Yes, for a few months. He loves it.
h Yes, please. I'd love some.

1b What color is Tuesday?

Reading synesthesia

1 Read about Mark and answer the questions.

1 Is synesthesia a disease?

_____

2 What happens when people have synesthesia?

_____

3 Does it affect Mark's life at all?

_____

4 How is Mark's synesthesia different from Kandinsky's?

_____

5 What's the most frequent example of synesthesia?

_____

6 Which part of the body is involved in synesthesia?

_____

2 Underline words in the text connected to the senses. Decide if they are nouns or verbs. Then use some of the words to complete these sentences.

1 I don't like the _____ of bananas.

2 When my cat _____ a bird singing, it gets very excited.

3 Most people's _____ gets worse as they get older.

4 Our sense of _____ is most sensitive in our fingertips.

5 Animal noses have a highly developed sense of _____ compared to humans.

What color is Tuesday?

My name is Mark, and I have synesthesia. It's not a disease (although I think it sounds like one) and it doesn't really have any serious effects on my day-to-day life, but it is a strange condition. Synesthesia happens when two or more of your senses get mixed up. So in my case, for example, I taste words. My sense of taste works even when I'm not eating anything, but when I hear or read certain words. For me, the word "box" tastes like eggs. That's just one example, of course. I'm reading one of the Sherlock Holmes stories at the moment and "Sherlock" is another "egg" word!

There are a lot of famous people with synesthesia. Two are the artist Wassily Kandinsky and the musician Stevie Wonder. Unfortunately for me, I only share my synesthesia with them, not any great artistic skills. I read that Kandinsky's synesthesia mixed color, hearing, touch, and smell. I don't think I'd like that. It seems very complicated.

My sister is synesthetic too, and she sees words in color. So when she sees the word "Tuesday" or just thinks of the word "Tuesday," she gets the feeling of "brown." Actually that kind of synesthesia, where the days of the week are colored, is the most common type. I read somewhere that synesthesia is connected to the way our brains develop language and that there's a link between sounds and shapes. I don't understand the idea very well, but it sounds fascinating.

Grammar questions

3 Write the missing word in each question. Then write the answers.

1 What condition Mark have?

    _____

    _____

2 else in his family has the same condition?

    _____

    _____

3 sense gives Mark problems?

    _____

    _____

4 synesthesia mixes color, hearing, touch, and smell?

    _____

    _____

5 What color Mark's sister associate with "Tuesday"?

    _____

    _____

4 Pronunciation direct questions

a ▶ 02 Listen and repeat the questions from Exercise 3. Pay attention to your intonation.

b ▶ 03 Read the questions with the correct intonation. Then listen and check.

1 Who's your favorite writer?

2 What kind of job do you do?

3 Where do you usually go on vacation?

4 What do you like to do on weekends?

5 How many languages do you speak?

6 How much TV do you watch?

5 Dictation questions

▶ 04 Listen and write the questions. Then complete the answers for yourself to see if you have synesthesia.

1 _____

  _____

  YOU: _____

2 _____

  _____

  YOU: _____

3 _____

  _____

  YOU: _____

4 _____

  _____

  YOU: _____

6 Write indirect questions for these direct questions.

1 What time is it?

  Can _____

2 What's your zip code?

  Could _____

3 Are the banks open today?

  Can _____

4 Where do I catch the downtown bus?

  Do _____

5 How does this machine work?

  Can _____

6 How long will you be here?

  Do _____

7 Is there a reduced price for students?

  Could _____

8 Why are you taking six classes?

  Can _____

Vocabulary feelings

7 Complete the sentences with one word from each pair.

anger / angry	lucky / luck
brave / bravery	powerful / power
happy / happiness	sad / sadness

1 Good _____ in your new job!

2 I'm always _____ on Sunday morning when I know I can get up late.

3 I have no _____ to do anything. I'm not the boss.

4 I feel _____ when I read about some people's difficult lives.

5 I think people who work with dangerous animals are very _____ .

6 I try not to get _____ when things go wrong.

1c Video games

Listening video games

1 How much do you know about video games? Match the names (1–4) with the types of game (a–d).

1 Super Mario ____
2 The Sims ____
3 Minecraft ____
4 Dragon Quest ____

a building adventure game
b life simulation game
c fantasy role play game
d sports and puzzle game

2 ▶ 05 Listen to an excerpt from a radio program about video games. Circle the correct option (a–c).

1 Millions of people ____ regularly play video games.
   a around the world
   b in the U.S.
   c in the U.K.

2 One of the main features of many video games is that the player chooses a new ____.
   a identity
   b life
   c team

3 Sometimes the character can be a powerful ____.
   a animal
   b leader
   c superhero

4 The university team's results suggest that our ideas about video games are ____.
   a correct
   b dangerous
   c wrong

5 Players like to choose identities that are ____ their own personalities.
   a different from
   b similar to
   c the same as

3 ▶ 05 Listen again. Answer the questions.

1 What did the team at the University of Essex want to do?
   _____

2 If you play The Sims, what kind of identity do you have?
   _____

3 What feelings do video games increase in players?
   _____

4 Vocabulary extra phrasal verbs

Look at the audioscript on page 100 to see how these phrasal verbs are used. Then replace the bold verbs with the correct forms of the phrasal verbs.

find out	turn into	go on	turn out

1 Your kitten **is becoming** a big fat cat! _____

2 What a mess! What**'s happening** here? _____

3 The police hope to **discover** who the thieves are. _____

4 It **seems** the problem with my hand is nothing serious. _____

5 Pronunciation extra of

▶ 06 When *of* links two nouns that often go together, it isn't stressed. Look at these words from the radio program. Do you think the word *of* is stressed? Listen and check.

1 millions of people
2 University of Essex
3 one of these games
4 a way of escaping

1d Making a good impression

Real life opening and closing conversations

1 Put the words in order to make statements and questions. Then circle O for ways of opening conversations and C for ways of closing conversations.

1 a / you / pleasure / to / it's / meet
   _____ . O C

2 card / give / let / me / my / you
   _____ . O C

3 myself / may / introduce / I
   _____ ? O C

4 stay / touch / in / let's
   _____ . O C

5 you / to / talking / good / been / it's
   _____ . O C

6 you / to / very / I'm / meet / pleased
   _____ . O C

2 Complete this conversation with four of the sentences from Exercise 1.

W: Good morning! ¹ _____
   My name is Will Marr.
G: How do you do? I'm Grace Larsen.
W: ² _____
   Grace. Are you a colleague of Dan's? ʼ
G: Yes, I am, actually. We're both working on this project.
   […]
W: Well, Grace, ³ _____
   I'm very interested in your ideas.
G: Thanks. ⁴ _____
   You can reach me at this number.
W: OK, thanks.

3 Use prepositions to complete these ways of talking about what you do.

1 I work _____ a design company.
2 I mostly work _____ special projects.
3 I'm an administrator _____ Brown's Bank.
4 I'm _____ Customer Services.
5 I'm looking _____ a new job at the moment.
6 I'm a student _____ City College.

4 Pronunciation short questions

a Match the comments (1–5) with the questions (a–e) to make short conversations.

1 I'm a colleague of Dan's.   ○   ○ a Can you?
2 She is one of our best customers. ○ ○ b Do you?
3 I work in our main office.   ○   ○ c Is she?
4 It's one of our biggest shops. ○   ○ d Oh, are you?
5 I can call you tomorrow.   ○   ○ e Oh, is it?

b ▶ 07 Now listen to the exchanges. Circle the questions where the speaker sounds interested.

c ▶ 08 Listen to the comments again. Reply to each comment with a question. Sound interested in each case.

5 Grammar extra auxiliary verbs in short questions and answers

> **AUXILIARY VERBS IN SHORT QUESTIONS AND ANSWERS**
>
> We use the auxiliary verbs *be* and *do* along with modal verbs to make short questions and short answers. (*Be* and *do* can also be main verbs.)
>
> | Auxiliary verbs | Examples |
> | --- | --- |
> | *be (am, are, is)* | *Are you? Yes, I am.* |
> | modal verb (*can, should,* etc.) | *Can she? No, she can't.* |
> | simple present (*do, does*) | *Do you? No, I don't.* |
> | present continuous (*am, is, are*) | *Are they? Yes, they are.* |

Write short questions or short answers in response to these comments.

1 I'm learning Greek at the moment.
   _____

2 This paint is selling very well.
   _____

3 Do you think you can win?
   Yes, _____

4 Can you see what's happening?
   No, _____

5 My colleagues are excited about this.
   _____

6 Listen and respond meeting people for the first time

▶ 09 Listen to comments from conversations where people meet for the first time. Respond with your own words. Then compare your response with the model answer that follows.

> *Hello, how are you? My name's Grace Larsen.*

> *I'm very pleased to meet you. I'm Alberto Costa.*

1e About us

Writing a business profile

1 Writing skill criteria for writing: text type, style, reader, purpose, and structure

a Read the excerpts from business communications. Circle the correct option.

1 text type: *letter* / *website*

> I'm pleased to inform you that we are offering a new range of services.

2 style: *formal* / *informal*

> **Check out our new range!
> We think it's really cool!**

3 reader: *known* / *not known*

> Please note the following changes to your account.

4 purpose: *to advertise a product* / *to give information*

> Our clients are national and international companies.

b Read the information from a business profile. Match the sentences (a–c) with the headings (1–3).

Intersect Design

1 About our work | 2 Satisfied customers | 3 About us

___ **a** "We always get fantastic results when we use Intersect." — *Blacks International*

___ **b** At the moment, we are developing a new logo for a national radio station.

___ **c** We are a design company with twenty years of experience.

2 Rewrite the sentences by putting the words in parentheses in the correct position. There is sometimes more than one possibility.

1 I am working on a new product. (this year)

_____

2 I can help you with new projects. (also)

_____

3 We are advising a national company. (currently)

_____

4 We are completing a major contract. (at this time)

_____

5 We have offices in all major cities. (in addition to this)

_____

6 We work in television. (too)

_____

3 Checking accuracy

Find and correct ten spelling mistakes in this profile.

1	_____	6	_____
2	_____	7	_____
3	_____	8	_____
4	_____	9	_____
5	_____	10	_____

I am a freelance designar in the fashion industry. I also work as a consultant for a sportswear manufacturer. My especial areas of interest include working with natural textiles and dies. I am currently developing a range of baby clothes that are non-alergic.

Outside work, I have a pasion for abstract art, especially the colorfull works of Kandinsky. I am continualy trying to improve my own skills as a paintor.

freelance (adj) /friːlæːns/ doing work for different organizations rather than working all the time for one

Wordbuilding adjective + noun collocations

> ▶ **WORDBUILDING adjective + noun collocations**
> Some adjectives and nouns often go together.
> *national identity, vegetarian food*

1 Complete the adjective + noun collocations in the sentences with words from the box. There is one extra noun.

Americans	clothes	culture	food
identity	impression	media	

1 My first _____ of Sue in the interview was really positive.

2 The people in any country are usually connected by a feeling of national _____ .

3 Many Native _____ are working to keep their traditions alive.

4 The magazine focuses on popular _____ —TV, movies, music, and so on.

5 I keep in touch with old friends on social _____ .

6 My grandparents still like to eat traditional _____ , especially on the weekend.

2 Complete the adjective + noun collocations in the sentences with words from the box. There is one extra adjective.

famous	middle	positive	serious
special	vegetarian	worldwide	

1 The restaurant is a great place to go if you want to celebrate a _____ occasion.

2 We eat _____ food almost all of the time these days. We hardly eat any meat.

3 Try and keep a _____ view of the changes that are happening at work.

4 The company aims to sell its new product to a _____ market.

5 The magazines you read are just about the lives of _____ celebrities.

6 I need to ask Ryan some really _____ questions about his plans for the future.

Learning skills study routines

Learning English is easier and you are more successful when you follow a routine.

3 Draw a chart showing your waking hours for each day of the week. Write your activities under the times. Then choose two colors and block off times:
- when you are free to study
- when you can study at the same time as you do something else, e.g., read on the bus

	7 a.m.	8 a.m.	9 a.m.	10 a.m.	11 a.m.
Monday	coffee	bus	work		break

4 How long do these activities need? Write 5, 30 or 60 (minutes) next to each one.
- reviewing vocabulary ——
- listening ——
- reading a magazine or graded reader ——
- doing Workbook exercises ——
- doing interactive online exercises ——
- watching a DVD ——
- doing homework for class ——

5 Match activities from Exercise 4 with color-blocked times in your chart from Exercise 3.

6 Use your chart to work out a realistic study routine.

Check!

7 Fill in the spaces (1–5) and find a word that means "the connections and similarities between different countries."

1 You should always check this when you're doing a piece of written work.

2 A type of cap some Americans wear.

3 Somewhere to stay on vacation.

4 Black is associated with this in many countries.

5 A way of sending a message online.

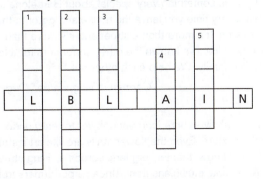

Unit 2 Performing

2a Street life

Reading La Rambla

1 Read what people say about La Rambla, a famous street in Barcelona. Write the names of the people.

1   Everything is new and exciting to
    _____ .
2   _____ likes the reaction he gets from people on La Rambla.
3   Living on La Rambla has had a positive effect on _____'s art.
4   _____ has been there for a long time.
5   _____ likes the variety of La Rambla.

2 Read what people say again. Are the sentences true (T) or false (F)? Or is there not enough information (N) in the text?

1   La Rambla attracts entertainers   T   F   N
    from around the world.
2   The performances are free   T   F   N
    to the public.
3   There is always some kind of   T   F   N
    performance happening on
    La Rambla.
4   La Rambla becomes quiet   T   F   N
    late at night.

66 This place is full of life, every hour of every day. I've felt much more alive since I came here. The area gives me lots of ideas. My paintings have gotten so much more interesting here. You can go out at night and always find something to do. I've never seen La Rambla without people. The place never sleeps. 99

Theo, portrait painter. Originally from Amsterdam.

66 I've just arrived and I've already heard about twenty different languages! It's awesome! There's so much going on. Everywhere you look there's some kind of performance. I especially like the puppeteers I saw this morning. I've never experienced anything like that before. 99

Kristen, language student. Originally from Chicago.

66 There is something very special about Barcelona and especially La Rambla. Every time you leave the house and go onto the street, you find some friends. It's more than a street and it's more than simply performing. It's a way of life. I've known the other performers for a long time now— they're like family. We help each other out. 99

Carmen, "living statue." Originally from Colombia.

66 I haven't lived here long enough yet to really understand it. But it's a fantastic mixture. Even the flower stalls are like art installations. You can see, I don't know, theater, jugglers, acrobats, living statues, tango dancers from Argentina, musicians from Africa … performers from all around the world. 99

Tara, singer. Originally from London.

66 We've been here for a few months. We love this street. There's entertainment on every corner. And when we play and maybe ten people start dancing—it's beautiful. It's a great place. 99

Alvaro, musician. Originally from Angola.

3 Find words for these performers in the article about La Rambla.

1 _____   2 _____

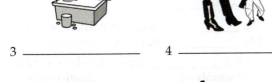

3 _____   4 _____

Grammar present perfect

4 Underline the present perfect verbs in the article about La Rambla. How many are there?

5 Complete the sentences with the present perfect form of the verbs, and *for* or *since* where necessary.

1 We _____ (be) here _____ a few weeks. We love everything we _____ (see) so far.

2 I _____ (perform) every night _____ I got here, and the crowds are great.

3 We _____ (never / have) so much success before.

4 My friend _____ (live) here _____ a couple of months, and now I _____ (decide) to join her.

5 I _____ (always / want) to sing in public, and now I can. _____ I came here, I _____ (become) more confident.

6 I _____ (not / hear) this music before. It's quite unusual.

6 Rewrite the sentences adding *already*, *just*, or *yet*.

1 Have you seen *Billy Elliot*?

_____

2 Don't book me a ticket. I've bought mine.

_____

3 I can't meet you later. I haven't finished my work.

_____

4 We've been to see Lady Gaga. Wow!

_____

5 I arrived this morning and I've seen dozens of performances.

_____

6 I'm not sure what that means! I've started learning Spanish.

_____

7 Pronunciation weak forms

▶ 10 Listen and practice the sentences from Exercise 6.

Vocabulary musical styles

8 Circle the correct option.

1 This music makes me happy with its *cheerful* / *sad* tune.

2 It's different from anything you've ever heard before. It's very *catchy* / *unusual*.

3 I like dancing to *lively* / *tuneless* music like this.

4 A *catchy* / *lively* tune is one you can't stop singing once you've heard it.

5 This kind of music gets boring and *repetitive* / *unusual* after you've heard it a few times.

6 It's a good song, but it makes me feel *interesting* / *sad*.

7 A lot of people have bought this record, but I think it's *cheerful* / *tuneless*.

8 The way this singer uses her voice is really exciting and *interesting* / *repetitive*.

2b One of a kind

Vocabulary emotions

1 Complete the sentences with these words.

bad mood	cheer up	cry	cry
laugh	laughing	smile	smile

1 I watched a really sad movie this weekend. It made me _____ .
2 I can't stop _____ at the joke my brother told me.
3 _____ ! It's not the end of the world.
4 The situation was so strange we didn't know whether to _____ or _____ .
5 Was something wrong yesterday? You seemed to be in a _____ .
6 Have you noticed? When you _____ at people, they _____ back.

Listening man on a wire

2 ▶ **11** Listen to two friends, Robin and Judy, talking about the photo on page 15. Are the sentences true (T) or false (F)?

1 Philippe Petit is a circus performer. T F
2 Petit has walked between towers in several countries. T F
3 It took Petit six years to organize the World Trade Center performance in New York. T F
4 He was on the wire at the World Trade Center for eight minutes. T F

3 ▶ **11** Listen again and complete the sentences. Sometimes there is more than one word.

1 Have you _____ this guy, Philippe Petit?
2 He _____ some amazing things.
3 He _____—on a wire—across the towers of Notre Dame.
4 I wonder what that _____ like?
5 He _____ to do the New York walk in 1968.
6 He _____ back and forth eight times!
7 They _____ a movie about him.

Grammar present perfect and simple past

4 Match the questions (a–b) with the answers (1–8). Then complete the questions and answers with the present perfect and simple past form of the verbs in parentheses.

a When _____ (be) the last time something really _____ (make) you laugh?
b What _____ you _____ (decide) to do for your vacation next week?

1 I can't remember! I _____ (not / laugh) for ages. ____
2 Actually, some friends _____ (invite) me to their house. ____
3 Just last night—I _____ (see) a really funny program on TV. ____
4 I'm not sure. I _____ (not / think) about it yet. ____
5 I _____ (book) a trip to Miami online last night. ____
6 We _____ (see) a comedian last week. He _____ (be) very funny. ____
7 Well, I _____ (just / finish) watching *Bridesmaids*—I _____ (laugh) through the whole movie. ____
8 A friend _____ (buy) me tickets for a music festival. It sounds like fun. ____

5 Complete the paragraph with the present perfect and simple past form of the verbs in the list.

be	begin	feel	go	have
learn	make	speak	not / study	understand

I [1] _____ learning Spanish about a year ago. I really enjoy the classes. When I [2] _____ at school, I [3] _____ any languages. So at first, I [4] _____ a little nervous. But I [5] _____ so much already! And I [6] _____ to Mexico twice on vacation. I [7] _____ lots of mistakes the first time I [8] _____ to someone, but they [9] _____ me. Most of my classmates [10] _____ the same kind of experiences at one time.

6 Pronunciation weak forms

▶ **12** Listen and repeat the sentences. Remember that the verb *have* is not stressed in present perfect statements.

1 My sister has been to *Wicked* three times.
2 I haven't had time to get groceries this week.
3 My friends and I have started learning Spanish.
4 Everybody has done the homework except me!
5 Hurry up! The performance has already started.
6 The performers have rehearsed the show for three weeks.

7 Vocabulary extra performing

a Circle the correct verbs.

1 (do / play) an instrument
2 (sing / tell) a joke
3 (give / star) a speech
4 (make / sing) karaoke
5 (give / make) an album
6 (make / write) a play
7 (tell / star) in a movie

b Write sentences with expressions from Exercise 7a.

1 Actors *star in movies.* _____
2 Authors _____
3 Comedians _____
4 Musicians _____
5 Ordinary people _____
6 Politicians _____
7 Rock bands _____

8 Dictation performing

▶ **13** Listen and write the sentences. Then decide if they are true for you.

1 _____
2 _____
3 _____
4 _____
5 _____
6 _____

"When I see three oranges, I juggle; when I see two towers, I walk."

Philippe Petit, high-wire artist, 1974

2c Life in a day

Listening a movie review

1 ▶ **14** Listen to a review of the movie *Life in a Day*. Answer the questions.

1 Why is the documentary called *Life in a Day*?
_____

2 What kind of documentary is it?
_____

3 Who filmed it?
_____

4 Are there any big stars in it?
_____

5 Whose idea was it?
_____

6 Where can you see it?
_____

2 ▶ **14** Listen again. Write the information.

1 the date of the documentary
_____

2 the length of the documentary
_____

3 the number of cameras
_____

4 the number of countries that received cameras
_____

5 the hours of footage
_____

6 the number of video clips
_____

7 the number of countries that sent footage
_____

> **footage** (n) /ˈfʊtɪdʒ/ sequence of images on film
> **shot** (v) /ʃɒt/ past participle of *shoot*: to record on film

3 What is the reviewer's opinion of the documentary? Circle one option (a–c).

a It's an unusual idea, but in the end it's a boring movie.

b It's one of the best movies she's ever seen.

c It's an interesting idea that has mainly succeeded.

Word focus *kind*

4 Is *kind* in these lines from the movie review an adjective (A) or a noun (N)?

1 "The experimental documentary *Life in a Day* is an unusual kind of film." ____

2 "What kind of picture do we get?" ____

3 "… people doing something kind for a neighbor …" ____

5 Complete the exchanges with these expressions.

certain kinds of	How kind	kind of
the right kind	the same kind	What kind of

1 A: _____ movies do you enjoy?
  B: Anything really, except horror movies. I've never liked them very much.

2 A: Rosa is going to help me with my Spanish homework.
  B: Oh, that's _____ her. Her Spanish is perfect!

3 A: How's your new job?
  B: Fine, thanks. It's _____ of work I've done before.

4 A: What's _____ of gasoline for the car?
  B: It's unleaded—that's the one with the green sticker.

5 A: I've made you a cake.
  B: Oh! _____ of you! It looks delicious.

6 A: Have you bought the tickets yet?
  B: Yes—there are _____ seats you have to book in advance.

2d What's on?

Real life choosing an event

1 Complete each suggestion in one or two ways. Refer to page 28 of the Student Book for expressions for choosing an event.

1 _____ see a movie tonight?
_____

2 _____ seeing a movie tonight?

2 Respond to this suggestion in three ways.

"Let's go to the MegaScreen—the new Russell Crowe movie is on."

_____

_____

_____

3 Write questions for these answers.

1 _____
There's a jazz concert at the City Hall.

2 _____
I think it's by Abi Morgan.

3 _____
It's got that guy who was in *Lost*.

4 _____
There's a late show at 11 p.m.

5 _____
It's the story of a young boy who loves dancing.

Vocabulary describing performances

4 Rewrite the sentences about performances as comments using these words. You can use the words in bold more than once.

absolutely	awful	boring	disappointing
good	hilarious	really	very

1 It was the funniest show you've ever been to.
It was absolutely hilarious.

2 It was the worst concert you've ever been to.
_____

3 You fell asleep during the play.
_____

4 The exhibition was better than average.
_____

5 You expected the performance to be better.
_____

5 Pronunciation intonation with *really*, *absolutely*, etc.

▶ 15 Listen and repeat the sentences. Pay attention to your intonation.

6 Grammar extra adjectives ending in *-ed* and *-ing*

▶ **ADJECTIVES ENDING IN *-ED* and *-ING***

We use the present participle and past participle of some verbs as adjectives: *bore → bored → boring*

-ed adjectives describe a person's state: *I'm bored. I was amazed.*

-ing adjectives describe the characteristics of a thing or person: *It was boring. They were amazing.*

Complete the sentences with the *-ed* or *-ing* form of these verbs.

amaze	bore	depress
disappoint	fascinate	move

1 With so many choices, how can you say you're _____ ?

2 Those acrobats were _____ . I don't know how they do that.

3 To be honest, I felt _____ by the lack of originality.

4 It's impossible not to be _____ by such beautiful music.

5 Another movie about terrible childhoods? How _____ !

6 What a _____ play that was! I'm still thinking about it now.

7 Listen and respond talking about events

▶ 16 Listen to the questions. Respond with a comment. Use your own words. Then compare your response with the model answer that follows.

Do you feel like going to the theater on Friday night?

Yeah, why not?

2e A portrait of an artist

Writing a review

1 Writing skill linking ideas

a Read the sentences about the Indian musician Ravi Shankar. Circle the correct answer(s).

1 He gave George Harrison, of the Beatles, some lessons on the sitar in 1968 and, *even though / because of this*, his music became more popular in the UK.

2 *Although / While* he was still young in his mind in his 90s, his body was too frail to play an instrument.

3 *Despite / In spite of* his age, he enjoyed music by artists such as Lady Gaga.

4 English music is written down. *In contrast, / For that reason,* Indian music is often improvised.

5 He appreciated most art forms, *but / so* he didn't like electronic music.

b Rewrite the sentences with the words in parentheses. Make any changes to verbs and punctuation as necessary.

a Even though he was from a classical Indian background, he'd had mainstream success in the West.
(despite)
_____
_____

b In 1956, he began playing Indian classical music on tour in Europe. That increased its popularity.
(because of this)
_____
_____

c He died in 2012 but his music is still popular today.
(although)
_____
_____

d He loved Matisse and Picasso. Nevertheless, he didn't believe in owning art.
(while)
_____
_____

e In spite of not knowing much about classical Indian music, I love his work.
(although)
_____
_____

2 Complete the sentences with the correct form of the verbs in parentheses. Then decide which sentences (a–e) from Exercise 1b go in the boxes. Write the complete review below.

1 Ravi Shankar was a classical Indian musician who _____ (have) huge success over many decades.

2 I _____ (follow) his work since I _____ (see) him on TV a few years ago. ☐

3 This _____ (begin) decades ago when he _____ (meet) George Harrison, of the Beatles. ☐

4 I enjoy the music he _____ (make) up until he passed away. ☐

5 I like it because it _____ (sound) beautiful and unusual to me. It's really different from Western music.

6 There _____ (recently be) an explosion in the kind of music we can hear, and I enjoy it all!

Wordbuilding noun and verb → noun

1 Complete the words that describe what people do.

1 artist, tour_____
2 actor, direct_____ , entertain_____ , paint_____
3 contestant, consult_____ , particip_____
4 musician, comed_____ , magic_____ , librar_____ , politic_____

2 These verbs all take the same suffix. Which one?

dance	design	learn	photograph	review
sell	sing	speak	teach	train

3 Complete the sentences with nouns (singular or plural) from Exercises 1 and 2.

1 A _____ helps you find books to borrow.
2 Van Gogh is one of my favorite _____ .
3 A lot of _____ visit New York, especially in the summer.
4 This is a great black-and-white image by a local _____ .
5 The TV show is a singing competition for _____ under the age of 16.

Learning skills mistakes

Making mistakes is part of learning. Thinking about mistakes in different categories can help you.

4 Look at these types of mistakes. Try to write down an example of each kind of mistake.

• mistakes you make because you haven't learned the correct word or structure yet
_____

• mistakes that are common to all learners with the same first language as you
_____

• mistakes that are "yours"—things you personally have problems with
_____

• mistakes that mean people can't understand your message properly
_____

5 Do you make mistakes with any of these things? Write an example.

1 the verb tense in sentences like "I haven't met many people since I moved here."
_____

2 the verb form in constructions like "Listening to music helps me feel more cheerful."
_____

3 adjectives like *bored/boring*
_____

6 Keep a record of mistakes you make often. Think about what kind of mistake they are. Write down the correct language and try to remember it. But don't worry too much about the mistakes that don't affect how well people understand you. And don't worry if it takes a while to correct your mistakes.

Check!

7 Answer these questions. The first letter of each answer spells a word. What it is it?

1 You take these things with a camera.	1	
2 Actors, comedians, acrobats, singers, etc., are all _____ .	2	
3 Music from Jamaica.	3	
4 A style of music and dance from southern Spain.	4	
5 A large group of people who play musical instruments together.	5	
6 The title of one of Baz Luhrmann's movies.	6	
7 Someone who does clever tricks for an audience.	7	
8 All artists need to have lots of _____ about their work.	8	
9 Joining a club is a good way of making _____ friends.	9	
10 Things that make you happy put you in a _____ mood.	10	

3a Underwater

Underwater
Brian Skerry

1 Finding the oceanic whitetip shark is an experience I won't forget. This is one of the most dangerous sharks in the world, but its numbers are falling. They used to be common around the Bahamas, but most people say they haven't seen them for years. Just as we arrived there, some sports fishermen in the central Bahamas saw some oceanic whitetips when they were fishing for tuna. So I set aside sixteen days to go searching for them.

For the first few days we didn't see a thing. Then, on the fifth day, I was looking out from the bridge when I spotted a shark on the surface. The white tip of its dorsal fin was sticking out of the water, so I knew we had an oceanic whitetip. I quickly put on my wetsuit and jumped in the water. The shark was very curious about me and swam right up to me. It was about three meters long, and it even stayed around while we were putting the cage in the water. I got some great pictures! That was really the high point of the assignment.

2 At the end of the assignment, after a year of work, we were going after the great hammerhead shark. This species is so elusive that there are hardly any pictures of it. For the entire first week, the weather was appalling and it was impossible to dive. It was very frustrating. Then, on the eighth day, my assistant had to fly home because his mother was seriously ill.

Suddenly, I was working alone as well as trying to deal with the bad weather. That was definitely the worst moment on the assignment. It is so important to have a really good assistant with you. Without him there, my workload more than doubled. While I was trying to decide what to do, the weather unexpectedly improved and I got a couple of not-bad days! And on one of those days, everything clicked and I got some great pictures of a hammerhead. I was lucky.

Reading on assignment

1 Read the stories by Brian Skerry about his year-long assignment photographing sharks. Match the number of the story (1 and 2) with the question (a and b).

  a What was one of your worst experiences covering this story? ____

  b What was one of your best experiences covering this story? ____

2 These statements are true for one or both of Skerry's stories. Write W (whitetip), H (hammerhead), and B (both).

  1 The sharks were difficult to find. _____

  2 Bad weather made it almost impossible to do any work. _____

  3 Some fishermen told Skerry where the sharks were. _____

  4 Skerry had to work without an assistant. _____

  5 Skerry got into the water as soon as he saw a shark. _____

  6 The shark spent some time swimming close to Skerry. _____

  7 Skerry was pleased with the photos he took. _____

3 Find these words and expressions in the stories. Circle the correct option.

  1 spotted: *photographed / saw*

  2 high point: *best moment / top of the boat*

  3 deal with: *survive / solve the problem*

  4 workload: *amount of work you have to do / problems*

  5 doubled: *increased by twice as much / increased by three times as much*

  6 clicked: *was quiet / was successful*

bridge (n) /brɪdʒ/ part of a boat or ship where the captain normally stands
dorsal fin (n) /ˈdɔːrsəl fɪn/ the part of a shark's back that sticks up
wetsuit (n) /ˈwetsuːt/ rubber clothes for water sports
elusive (adj) /ɪˈluːsɪv/ extremely rare and difficult to see

Grammar simple past and past continuous

4 Write questions for these answers. Use the information from the stories.

1 When _____ ?
   When they were fishing for tuna.
2 When _____ ?
   While he was looking out from the bridge.
3 How _____ ?
   Because the white tip of its dorsal fin was sticking out of the water.
4 What _____ ?
   They were going after the great hammerhead shark.
5 What _____ ?
   Skerry's assistant flew home.
6 What _____ ?
   He was trying to decide what to do.

5 Complete the sentences with the correct form of the verbs in parentheses.

1 We _____ a shark when we
   _____ .
   (see / surf)
2 I _____ back into the boat
   when I _____ my camera into the
   water.
   (climb / drop)
3 It _____ a beautiful morning. The
   sun _____ over the horizon and
   the fish _____ .
   (be / come up / jump)
4 It _____ to rain while we
   _____ a really good sequence.
   (start / film)
5 We _____ in the boat, quickly
   _____ our equipment, and
   _____ home.
   (get / pack up /go)
6 While we _____ back to land,
   the wind suddenly _____ a lot
   stronger.
   (sail / get)

6 Pronunciation *d* and *t* after *-ed* endings

a Underline the verbs with *-ed* endings and the word that follows.

1 I climbed down the side of the boat.
2 We decided to go for a swim.
3 The shark looked dangerous, so I swam away.
4 I dropped Tom's camera into the water.
5 I learned to swim when I was five.
6 The sun came out and the sea turned deep blue.

b ▶ 17 Listen and repeat the sentences.

Vocabulary describing experiences

7 Complete the sentences with these adverbs. Sometimes you can use more than one adverb.

badly	carefully	easily	fortunately
immediately	noisily	safely	suddenly

1 The shark _____ turned and
   swam toward me.
2 The lake wasn't very big, so we swam across it
   _____ .
3 I got out of the kayak very _____
   so that I didn't fall in the river.
4 The children ran _____ down the
   beach to the sea.
5 We dived into the water and
   _____ saw some beautiful fish.
6 I tried windsurfing, but I did it so
   _____ that I gave up after ten
   minutes.
7 I had an accident while I was jet-skiing, but
   _____ it wasn't serious.
8 When you're diving, you need to
   make sure you come up to the surface
   _____ .

3b Problems and rescues

Vocabulary at sea

1 Write the names of these things. They are all on Student Book pages 36–37.

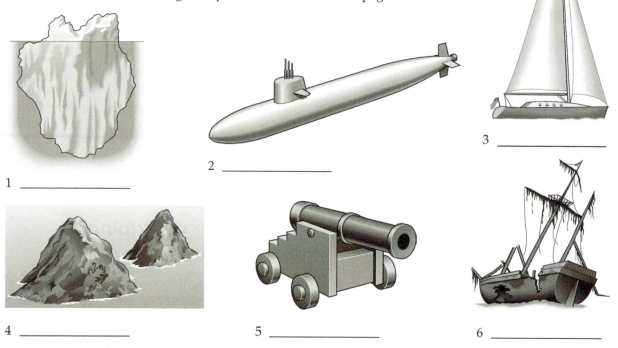

1 _____

2 _____

3 _____

4 _____

5 _____

6 _____

Listening Hurricane Mitch

2 What kind of landscape does the photo show? Circle one option (a–c).

a desert
b farmland
c forest

3 ▶ 18 You are going to listen to the introduction to a program about hurricanes. Check (✓) the words you think you will hear. Then listen and check.

clouds	destructive	flooded	ocean
powerful	rainfall	sand	tornado
tropical	waves	wet	winds

4 ▶ **18** Listen again. Circle the correct option (a–c).

1 Hurricanes begin in the _____ .
   a Atlantic Ocean
   b Indian Ocean
   c Pacific Ocean

2 There is a hurricane season _____ .
   a every month
   b every year
   c every ten years

3 Hurricane Mitch affected _____ .
   a North and South America
   b the Caribbean and South America
   c the Caribbean and Central America

4 _____ fell in one day in Honduras.
   a Six days' rain
   b Two months' rain
   c Two hundred days' rain

5 What happened to these things during Hurricane Mitch?

1 bridges
   _____

2 farmland
   _____

3 rivers
   _____

4 roads
   _____

5 sand
   _____

6 trees
   _____

Grammar past perfect

6 Change one verb in each sentence to the past perfect.

1 By the time the storm reached land, most residents left the area.
   _____

2 When people got back home, they were amazed at what happened.
   _____

3 In some places, before the hurricane there were trees, but now there was nothing.
   _____

4 Many roads and bridges disappeared by the end of the first day.
   _____

5 After the hurricane, there was a desert where people had farms.
   _____

6 It became clear how much changed when people saw the satellite images.
   _____

7 Complete the news item with the simple past and past perfect form of these verbs.

be	be able to	become
already / die	manage	try

Rescuers in Scotland [1]_____ to return twenty whales to the sea this weekend. The whales [2]_____ from a larger group that [3]_____ stuck on the beach. Several other whales [4]_____ before the rescuers [5]_____ help them. Earlier, the rescue team [6]_____ unsuccessfully to stop the whales from coming too close to the shore. The reason for the whales' behavior is not clear.

8 Dictation a rescue

▶ **19** Listen and write down information from a news item about the Coast Guard. Then put the sentences in order.

a _____
  _____

b _____
  _____

c _____
  _____

d _____
  _____

e _____
  _____

3c Bottled water

Listening water on tap?

WHO DRINKS THE MOST BOTTLED WATER?

Top ten markets by liters per person in 2006			
203	Italy	129	Germany
197	United Arab Emirates	126	Spain
191	Mexico	117	Lebanon
149	France	110	Switzerland
145	Belgium/Luxembourg	104	United States

1 Look at the information about bottled water. Where do people drink the most bottled water?

_____

2 ▶ 20 Listen to part of a radio program about Bundanoon, a bottled-water free town in Australia. Answer the questions.

1 Where does Bundanoon get its water from?

_____

2 What did the water company want to do?

_____

3 What had local businessman Huw Kingston done?

_____

4 What happened at the town meeting?

_____

5 When did environmental groups start to support the town?

_____

3 ▶ 20 Listen again. Complete the sentences.

1 The residents of Bundanoon were against the water company's plans because _____
_____ .

2 Huw Kingston wanted the town to _____
_____
and _____ .

3 A few residents heard about another Australian town that _____
_____ .

4 The residents discovered that the carbon footprint of bottled water _____
_____ .

5 If a visitor to Bundanoon wants some water,
_____

---

ban (v) /bæn/ prohibit
pioneer (n) /ˌpaɪəˈnɪər/ the first to do something
reusable (adj) /ˌriːˈjuːzəbl/ can be used more than once

Word focus *get*

4 Look at these sentences from the radio program. Replace the words in bold with four of these words. There is one extra word.

become	entered	met	obtain	received

1 And how did you **get** involved in the story?

_____

2 A few residents **got together** to investigate how we could go "bottled-water free."

_____

3 After they wrote about us, we **got** a lot of support from environmental movements.

_____

4 All the water in our town is free, so you can **get** it from the tap.

_____

5 Match the comments (1–5) with the responses (a–e).

1 How did you get on at the meeting? ____
2 This company wants to bottle the town's water. ____
3 How's the campaign going? ____
4 How did you get your picture in the papers? ____
5 What a crazy week! ____

a We just got in touch with the journalists about the campaign.
b I don't get it. Why do they want to do that?
c I know! I can't wait for things to get back to normal.
d Really well. They agreed to all of our suggestions.
e Things are getting better now that we've been on TV.

3d No way!

Real life telling stories

1 Complete the story with these words.

after   during   later   suddenly   then   while

Did I ever tell you about the time I went fishing with my girlfriend's father? [1] _____ the drive to the lake, he told me about all the huge fish he'd caught. [2] _____ half an hour of this, I wanted to go home. Anyway, we'd been on the lake for a couple of hours when [3] _____ , my fishing rod started to move. [4] _____ I was trying to bring the fish in, he was shouting, "It's massive, really big!" Thirty minutes [5] _____ , I still hadn't managed to get the fish in the boat. And [6] _____ I dropped my rod in the water. My girlfriend's father was horrified.

2 Grammar extra *when/while/as*

> ▶ **WHEN/WHILE/AS**
>
> We can use *when, while,* and *as* to show that two actions happened at the same time.
>
> Use *when* with a short action (simple past) which happened during a longer action:
> > *We were sitting in the boat when my fishing rod moved.*
>
> Use *while* for two longer actions:
> > *While I was trying to control it, he was shouting.*
>
> Use *as* for two short actions:
> > *As I stepped forward I dropped the rod.*

Circle the best option.

1   We were walking in the park *while / when* we heard a strange noise.
2   *As / While* I walked out my front door, I felt the rain.
3   *While / When* we were putting gas in the car, the sky was getting darker.
4   A dog was barking noisily *as / when* we were taking our exam.
5   We were talking about our plans *while / when* my phone rang.
6   *As / While* I got back home, the sun came out.

3 Pronunciation *was* and *were*

a ▶ 21 Listen and repeat the sentences you hear. Pay attention to how you say *was* and *were*.

b Now practice saying sentences 1, 3, and 5 from Exercise 2.

4 Listen and respond asking about things that happened

▶ 22 Listen to people talking about things that happened to them. Respond with a question. Use your own words. Then compare your response with the model answer that follows.

> *Did I ever tell you about the time we ran out of gas?*

> *No. Where were you going?*

3e What a weekend!

Writing a blog post

1 Jenna's computer has made a mess of her blog. Put the text in the correct order. Write numbers next to the lines.

Titanic Fanatics trip to Belfast

Well, that certainly was a weekend to remember! After months of
embarking on a new life. The entire experience was
<u>here</u>.
members of the *Titanic Fanatics Society*, and we unexpectedly
especially moving as I thought about all those heroic passengers
On Saturday morning, we made our way to the spectacular
completely packed, of course —nobody wanted to miss the centenary
planning, we finally made it to Belfast to see where the whole
bumped into some familiar faces on Friday evening, too. The hotel was
Wandering slowly through the authentically recreated cabins was
Titanic Belfast center. It was thrilling to see the place where
the *Titanic* was designed, built, and launched a century ago.
tragic *Titanic* story began. There were sixteen of us altogether, all
unforgettable, and you can see all my photos and read more
weekend.

a *1*
b _____
c _____
d _____
e _____
f _____
g *6*
h _____
i _____
j _____
k _____
l _____
m _____
n _____
o _____

2 Writing skill interesting language

a Match these words with the expressions Jenna used.

amazing	arrived in	exciting	full of people
sad	starting	went	met some friends

1 we finally **made it to** Belfast: _____

2 **tragic** story: _____

3 we **bumped into** some **familiar faces**:
_____

4 **packed:** _____

5 we **made our way** to: _____

6 **spectacular:** _____

7 **thrilling:** _____

8 **embarking on** a new life: _____

b Complete the sentences with some of the words Jenna used from Exercise 2a.

1 The new building is _____ .

2 I _____ my boss at the mall.

3 The bus is _____ during rush hour.

4 I got on the train and _____ to my seat.

5 I was surprised to see _____ at the exhibition.

3 Look at the words below. Find four words to describe:

1 a view: _____ , _____ ,
_____ , _____

2 an experience: _____ , _____ ,
_____ , _____

3 a place you are in: _____ ,
_____ , _____ , _____

4 ways of "going": _____ ,
_____ , _____ , _____

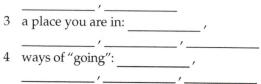

impressive packed exciting busy
magnificent exhilarating travel set off
crowded spectacular electrifying thrilling
take off move on fabulous full

4 Use these notes to write the second part of Jenna's blog.

- Saturday evening / got dressed up
- dinner / spectacular dining room
- whole thing / re-creation / dinner on the *Titanic*
- dining room / packed / thrilling / authentic costumes
- bumped into / people / earlier / joined
- food / amazing / whole thing / moving

Wordbuilding adverbs with -ly

> ▶ **WORDBUILDING adverbs with -ly**
>
> Some adverbs are formed by adding -ly to adjectives. Sometimes there is a spelling change.
> add -ly: loud → loud**ly**
> drop -e, add -ly: gentle → gent**ly**
> drop -y, add -ily: lucky → luck**ily**

1 Make adverbs from these adjectives.

close	easy	exact
final	immediate	incredible
natural	normal	professional
recent	unexpected	extreme

2 Complete these sentences using adjectives or adverbs from Exercise 1. Sometimes you can use more than one adverb or adjective.

1 When I saw the shark, I felt
_____ frightened!

2 We've had lots of visitors
_____ .

3 Jack always works in a very
_____ way.

4 We need to arrive at
_____ one o'clock.

5 Sue's underwater photos are just
_____ !

6 There were a lot of cars, but to our surprise, we were able to park
_____ .

Learning skills keeping a journal

3 Keeping a journal can help you remember everything. Look at the page from a journal and check (✓) the things the student has included.

- diagrams / drawings
- example sentences
- grammar
- how he/she feels about something
- listening
- other students
- questions for the teacher
- reading
- reminders to do things
- self-evaluation
- speaking
- test scores
- vocabulary
- writing

Nov. 3	8/10 in a vocabulary test! ☺
Nov. 6	
new words	shipwreck iceberg nearby edge
grammar	
reading	The reading text was difficult! Read it again over the weekend.
	Paola told me about going on her trip to Disney World—very funny.
sentence	I got back home at 11:30.
Nov. 10	We watched a DVD about water in India.

4 Circle the options which work best for you. Then try keeping a journal for a month.

1 type of journal: *notebook / computer-based / online blog*

2 entries: *every day / after every class / every week*

3 type of entry: *notes / a narrative / analytical*

4 focus: *what I learn / how I learn / strong points / weak points*

5 reread: *after each entry / every week / every two weeks*

Check!

5 All these words go with *water*. Which ones are in the word square? Use the clues to help you.

boiling	bottled	clean	cold	deep	dirty	fresh
rain	river	salt	sea	tap	running	hot

X	F	L	H	H	N	I	E	K	O
H	R	I	R	U	N	N	I	N	G
A	E	B	S	E	L	A	Z	B	I
R	S	O	Q	V	O	B	U	O	T
E	H	I	P	N	H	O	T	Y	S
O	A	L	Z	I	P	T	E	W	A
R	A	I	N	P	L	T	I	R	L
P	L	N	I	E	U	L	T	T	T
E	B	G	S	U	A	E	N	B	O
Y	U	V	C	O	L	D	X	R	U

1 It falls from the sky and you can collect it in a tank.

2 Some people only drink this kind, but it's expensive.

3 Lakes are almost always this kind of water.

4 When your home gets a continuous supply from pipes.

5 If you're in this kind of water, it means you have done something wrong.

6 This kind is needed to make a cup of tea.

7 The oceans and seas of the world are made of this.

8 When you don't like an idea, you pour this kind of water on it.

4a Future world

Wensday 8 nov.

Word focus *job* and *work*

1 Complete the sentences with the correct form of *job* or *work*.

1 The project will bring lots of new _____job_____ to the area.
2 Do you enjoy _____working_____ here?
3 How often do you take a day off from _____work_____?
4 How can you do three _____job_____ at once? That's impossible!
5 She has a lot to do at _____work_____ at the moment.
6 What's your _____job_____?
7 Phil and I _____work_____ in the same company. We both enjoy it.
8 I started my first _____job_____ when I was still at school. It was in a local store.

Listening **children of the future**

2 ▶ 23 Listen to four parents of young babies talking about their children's futures. Check (✓) the things the speakers (1–4) mention. You can check more than one thing for each speaker.

	1	2	3	4
education	✓			
environment				✓
health			✓	
home		✓		
languages				✓
work		✓		

3 ▶ 23 Listen again to the predictions the parents make about these things. Are they 100 percent sure (S) or not 100 percent sure (NS) of their predictions?

1 using a computer __S__
2 leaving school __S__
3 using robots __S__
4 driving electric cars __NS__
5 working full time __S__
6 living to be 100 __S__
7 effects of climate change __NS__
8 speaking Chinese __NS__

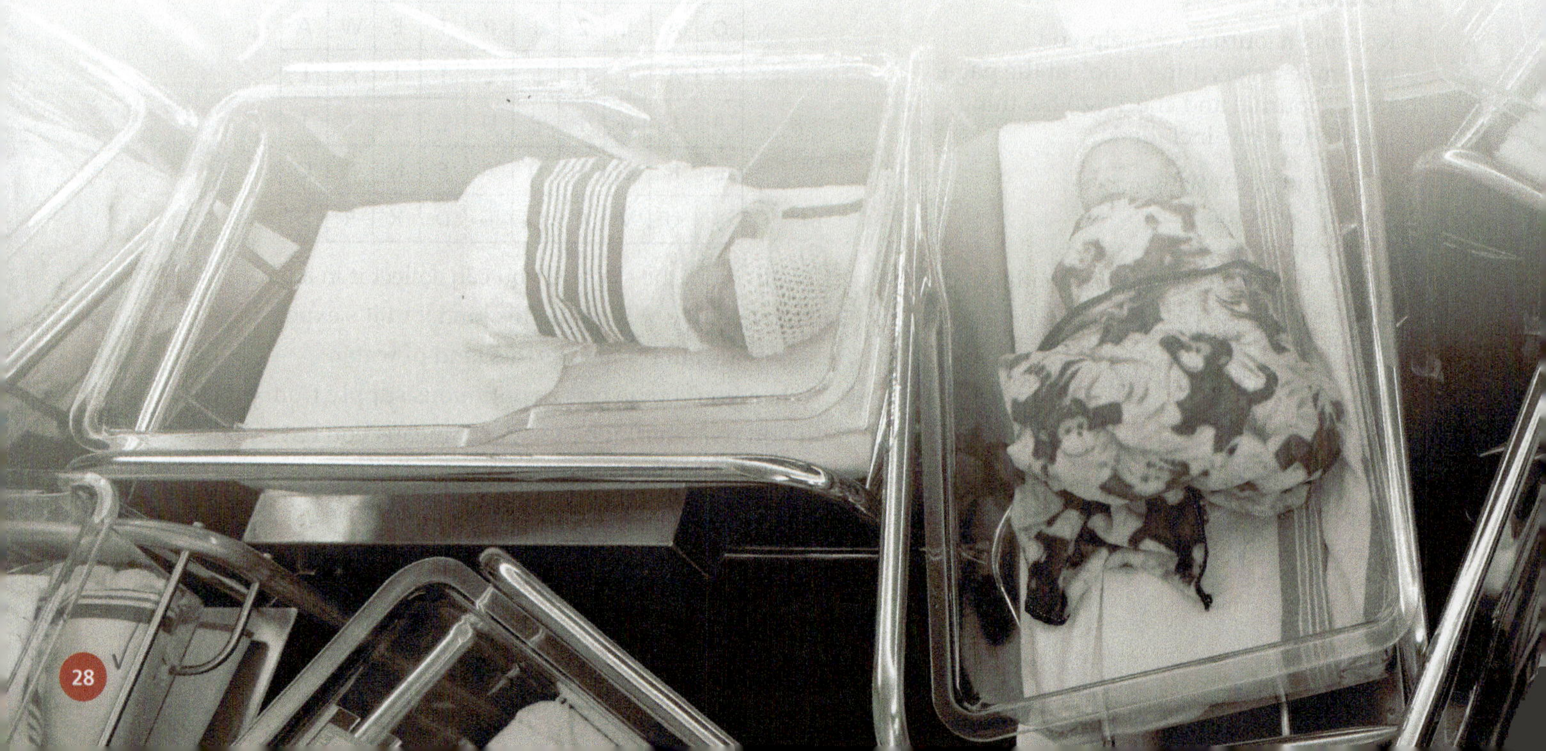

Grammar predictions

4 Complete the predictions with one word so that they are 100 percent sure. Sometimes more than one option is correct.

1 The world _will_ be a very different place in a few years' time. I'm sure of that.
2 He _won't_ (not) leave school at sixteen like I did.
3 Robots and computers _will_ take care of all the routine, boring things.
4 She _definitely_ won't work full-time.
5 They'll _certainly_ find cures for many of the health problems we face today.

5 Complete the predictions with one word so that they are NOT 100 percent sure. Sometimes more than one option is correct.

1 She'll _probably_ live to be a hundred.
2 She _might_ get sick at some point in her life.
3 This _could_ affect their world in ways we haven't imagined.
4 They _may_ not learn it at school.
5 That _could_ be a challenge!

6 Read the first sentence. Then circle the logical prediction (a or b).

1 We're planning to have a baby.
  (a) It might be a girl.
  b It will be a girl.
2 My son has a cold.
  a He may get better soon.
  (b) He'll get better soon.
3 People are living longer these days.
  (a) I could live to be a hundred.
  b I'll live to be a hundred.
4 Electric cars are on sale now.
  a Some people might buy them.
  (b) Some people will buy them.
5 Domestic robots can do more things than before.
  a Every home will have one.
  (b) They might become more popular.
6 My sister writes children's books.
  (a) Robots will never be able to do her job.
  b Robots might not do her job in the future.

7 Dictation predictions

▶ **24** Listen and write the six predictions. Then decide how much you agree with each one.
(✗ = disagree, ✓ = mostly agree, ✓✓ = completely agree)

1 _____ ☐
2 _____ ☐
3 _____ ☐
4 _____ ☐
5 _____ ☐
6 _____ ☐

4b Now what?

Vocabulary education

1 Complete the questions with these expressions. Then answer the questions.

become an apprentice	leave school
drop out of college	pass an exam
get a degree	retake an exam
go to university	stay in school

In your country:

1 At what age can you legally _____ _____ ?
_____

2 Do many teenagers _____ after compulsory education?
_____

3 What is the minimum grade you need to _____ ?
_____

4 How many times can you _____ _____ after you fail it?
_____

5 Do people _____ close to home or in other towns?
_____

6 Is it easy to _____ in a factory?
_____

7 How many years does it take to _____ _____ ?
_____

8 Do many people _____ and get a job instead?
_____

Reading going back

2 Look at the photo of Lorna. Decide which option you think is correct in each question. Then read the email on page 31 and check your ideas.

1 Is she in a bar or a café?
_____

2 Is she a waitress or a chef?
_____

3 Does she work there, or is she the owner?
_____

4 Is she in her twenties or her thirties?
_____

5 Is she single or married?
_____

3 Read Lorna's email again. Answer the questions.

1 Where is she from?
_____

2 Where has she been for the past year?
_____

3 Why is she writing to her brother?
_____

4 What does she think of Los Angeles?
_____

4 Correct the factual mistakes in these sentences.

1 Lorna's brother is finishing his apprenticeship soon.

_____

2 Lorna will be back in Vancouver next week.

_____

3 She's going to look for a new job in Los Angeles.

_____

4 She's found somewhere to live in Vancouver.

_____

5 She won't be able to stay with Brett.

_____

6 She promises to bring her brother to Hollywood.

_____

Hey little brother, how are you doing?

I bet you can't wait to leave school and start that apprenticeship. I can't remember if you got a place at Autofit or City Bridges …

Anyway, here's some news—I'm coming back after this job. Don't tell Mom yet—I want to surprise her. I'll be back in Vancouver in May or June, I think. The café I'm working in is losing customers and money, and two staff members are leaving next week! I'll be next, I bet … So I'm going to take a few months off and see what turns up back home. I could look for another job here, but after almost a year of waitressing I feel like doing something new. Los Angeles has been great, but I'm not going to stay here forever. I suppose I'll have to think about what I'm going to do in the long term at some point soon.

I'll need to find somewhere to live in Vancouver, that's the first thing. I guess you're going to stay at home with Mom. Apprentices don't earn much, do they? I was talking to Brett and he's staying on next year to do another course at college, or something, so I might be able to stay with him while I do some job-hunting. If that doesn't work out … well, I'll think of something! I may even move back to live with you and Mom! But at 25, I don't think that's such a good idea.

Anyway, this is just to let you know my plans, as far as they go at the moment! See you in a couple of months—I'll bring you a Hollywood mug!

Love,
Lorna
xxxx

Grammar future forms

5 Match the future forms in the sentences (1–8) with the uses (a–d).

1 We're going to see the *Futures* exhibition on Saturday. Do you want to come? ____

2 We're meeting at the door at one-thirty. ____

3 The office doesn't open until nine o'clock. ____

4 OK then, I'll see you later. Have a nice afternoon. ____

5 Did you hear? Bob and Vicky are getting married next summer. ____

6 I'm not going to continue with the course, I'm afraid. I don't have the time. ____

7 Don't forget—the clocks go back next weekend. ____

8 We can all go in the same car—we'll pick you up at ten. ____

a a plan or intention decided before the moment of speaking

b a decision made at the moment of speaking

c an event that follows a regular schedule or timetable

d a fixed arrangement to do something at a specified (or understood) time in the future

6 Look again at the uses of future forms in Exercise 5. Then write sentences using the appropriate form.

1 I / look for a new job (a)

_____

2 I / start my new job next week (d)

_____

3 I / meet you tonight (b)

_____

4 the bus / leave at eight o'clock (c)

_____

5 my friend / drop out of college (a)

_____

6 my friend / take an exam tomorrow (d)

_____

7 I / help you study (b)

_____

8 the exam / take place at the end of June (c)

_____

7 **Pronunciation extra** /l/

▶ 25 Listen to the sentences. Write the word from each sentence which includes the letter *l*. Repeat the sentences.

1	_____	4	_____
2	_____	5	_____
3	_____	6	_____

4c Looking ahead

Vocabulary pay and conditions

1 Circle the best option.

1 I'll see you at three. I can get off early because I'm on *flextime / overtime*.

2 It's hard to feel motivated when we haven't had a *bonus / pay raise* in seven years.

3 I love working in a clothing store, especially because they give *staff discounts / pension plans* on the products!

4 I'm doing really well, so I hope I get a *promotion / salary* soon.

5 I'm looking for *part-time work / wages* because we have a young family.

6 I won't be able to go traveling with you. I only get one week's *long hours / paid vacation* this year.

Listening radio interviews

2 ▶ 26 Circle the correct option (a–c). Then listen to part of a radio program and check.

1 How old are the people being interviewed?
  a less than fifteen years old
  b between twenty and thirty years old
  c more than forty years old

2 What do we call the occasion when you are given your university degree?
  a final meeting
  b graduation ceremony
  c leaving party

3 What do we call the occasion married couples celebrate every year?
  a engagement party
  b marriage ceremony
  c wedding anniversary

3 ▶ 26 Listen again. Are the sentences true (T) or false (F)?

1 The host talks about last week's   T   F
  program.

2 Anton doesn't want to settle down yet.   T   F

3 Anton's job pays well.   T   F

4 Carey is about to start university.   T   F

5 Carey isn't working at the moment.   T   F

6 Carey and Anton have both overcome   T   F
  challenges in their lives.

4 Answer the questions using information from the radio program.

1 What is the "internet generation"?
_____

2 What does Anton say about plans?
_____

3 Why does Carey believe you need an open mind?
_____

4 Why do you think the program is called *Turning 21*?
_____

5 Pronunciation extra *'ll*

a ▶ 27 The contracted form of *will* (*'ll*) is not stressed. Listen to these pairs of sentences. Which sentence do you hear first?

1 a We'll meet some of the "internet generation."
  b We meet some of the "internet generation."

2 a We'll find out what it means to be 21 today.
  b We find out what it means to be 21 today.

3 a We'll have my graduation ceremony.
  b We have my graduation ceremony.

4 a I'll try anything.
  b I try anything.

b ▶ 27 Listen again. Practice saying the sentences.

4d Would you mind ... ?

Vocabulary job requirements

1 Circle the best option.

1 Researchers need to be *creative / well organized* as they deal with lots of information.

2 Entrepreneurs need to be *methodical / self-confident* to be a success.

3 Farmers need to be *creative / independent* if they are self-employed.

4 Accountants need to be *energetic / methodical* because their work is very detailed.

5 Managers need to be *creative / well organized* when trying to solve problems.

6 Technicians need to be *conscientious / self-confident,* as their work can be routine.

2 Grammar extra predictions with *going to*

> **PREDICTIONS WITH *GOING TO***
>
> We can use *going to* to make a prediction based on something that means the speaker thinks it is certain to happen:
>
> *My company is in trouble. I'm going to lose my job.*

Match the situations (1–4) with the predictions (a–d).

1 I'm so nervous about this interview. ____

2 The interview was awful. ____

3 The other candidate was more experienced. ____

4 Your resume is really strong. ____

a They aren't going to offer me the job.

b She's going to get the job.

c You're going to get an interview.

d It's going to be a disaster.

Real life making and responding to requests

3 Use combinations of these words to complete the requests. You can use the words more than once.

all right it	be mind	can OK	could to	do will	if would	is you

1 _____ I borrow your phone?

2 _____ I used your computer?

3 _____ have a look at this application form?

4 _____ give your name?

5 _____ reading this letter for me?

4 Pronunciation weak and strong auxiliary verbs

▶ 28 Listen and repeat the exchanges you hear. Pay attention to the weak and strong auxiliary verbs.

5 Listen and respond answering questions

▶ 29 Listen to each question about a job application process. Respond with your own answer. Then compare your response with the model answer that follows.

> *Are you looking for a new job at the moment?*

> *Yes, I am actually.*

4e I am enclosing my resume

Writing a cover letter

1 Writing skill formal style

a Which of these things (a–d) is not a feature of formal letters?

   a concise sentences
   b formal phrases to begin sentences
   c contractions
   d standard phrases to open and close the letter

b Rewrite the phrases and sentences in the appropriate style for a cover letter.

1 Hi Mr. Brown,
_____

2 I saw your ad.
_____

3 Here's my application form.
_____

4 I'm a fun kind of person.
_____

5 I've done this kind of work before.
_____

6 Do you want to interview me soon?
_____

7 Send me an email or text me.
_____

8 All the best,
_____

2 Read the profile and the advertisement. Underline the sections in the advertisement that correspond to the profile information.

Profile: Manuel Santos

- enthusiastic
- hard-working
- enjoys working with people

Wants: a job in catering

Experience: restaurants, cafeterias (U.S., Brazil)

Availability: now

AROMA CAFÉS

| Home | About | Jobs |

We are an expanding chain of specialty cafés looking for outgoing, energetic servers.

- part-time position leading to full-time opportunity

You will be responsible for:

- serving customers
- maintaining stock
- maintaining a clean environment

Characteristics of ideal candidates are:

- some experience in catering or retail
- excellent communication skills
- hard-working and good under pressure
- authorized to work in the U.S.

Send application form and cover letter to:
Jim.Kapoor@aroma
Ref 119/XG Closing date October 31st

3 Write a cover email from Manuel Santos to go with the completed application form for this job.

_____
_____
_____
_____
_____
_____
_____
_____
_____
_____
_____
_____
_____
_____
_____
_____
_____
_____
_____
_____
_____

Wordbuilding prefix *re-*

1 Match the beginnings of the sentences (1–7) with the endings (a–g).

1 What a mess! I'll have to ____
2 After the hurricane, they had to ____
3 Apparently, most divorced people ____
4 Do we have to buy new gas bottles? Or can you ____
5 I lost my contacts list on my cell phone, but now it's ____
6 There are big changes at work—they are ____
7 I wasn't happy with my essay, so I decided to ____

a reappeared.
b rebuild many houses.
c redo all of this.
d refill these?
e remarry within a few years.
f restructuring the organization of the whole company.
g rewrite the introduction and the conclusion.

2 Some verbs that start with *re-* have the idea of "back" or "again," but we don't usually use the verb without the prefix. Look at the example. Complete the sentences with verbs from the box. Use the correct form.

| recover repeat reply return review |

1 Sam was really sick, but he's _____*recovering*_____ now.
2 Can you _____ what you said? I didn't catch it all.
3 I'll _____ to my emails later. I'm in a hurry now.
4 It's always a good idea to _____ your work before you hand it in.
5 These new shoes don't fit, so I'm going to _____ them.

Learning skills recording new words (1)

3 Look at the strategies (a–e). Write notes for these words. Which information helps you remember how to use the word?

hard-working: _____

full-time: _____

enclose: _____

a how to say it in your own language
b how to pronounce it
c what kind of word it is (noun, adjective, verb, adverb)
d how to use it (example sentences)
e when to use it (in writing or speaking)

4 Organizing new words into groups can help you remember them. How many words from Unit 4 can you add to each group?

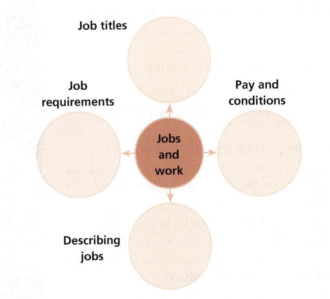

Job titles

Job requirements

Pay and conditions

Jobs and work

Describing jobs

Check!

5 Answer these questions. Then rearrange the first letters of the answers to give the name of a country from Unit 4.

1 If you don't like your current job, look for a _____ one.
2 Something every child has when they think about their future: _____
3 If you plan to do something, you _____ to do it.
4 You can learn how to be an engineer here: _____
5 All employers want their employees to be this: _____

	1	2	3	4	5
Letters					
Word					

Unit 5 Well-being

5a Natural foods

Word focus *make*

1 ▶ 30 Listen to two people discussing a cooking dilemma. Complete the sentences.

1 Are you going to ___make___ something?
2 Because it will help you make _____
_____ _____ .
3 I still want to make _____ _____
_____ _____ .
4 I could make cheese soufflé or prawn curry or just a _____ _____ ?
5 Can I make _____ _____ ?
6 All this talk about food is making _____
_____ !

2 Add the expressions from Exercise 1 to the patterns (1–5).

1 **make** (to produce something): *lunch,*
_____

2 **make** + noun (an action, to do something):
a plan, a mess, _____

3 **make** + *somebody* + noun (to do something for someone): *me a sandwich, you a drink,*
_____

4 **make** + *somebody* + adjective (to cause something): *me sick, you better,*
_____

5 other expressions: *make something up, make sense,* _____

3 Complete the sentences with expressions from Exercises 1 and 2.

1 I'm feeling pretty stressed. I have to
_____ for ten people today!
2 Look at this kitchen! Why must you always
_____ when you cook?
3 I can't eat much chocolate. It _____
_____—it gives me a headache.
4 Are you thirsty? Can I _____
_____ ?
5 I don't understand this recipe at all. It just doesn't _____ .
6 I don't know what to get for dessert. I can't
_____ .

Listening **bush tucker**

4 ▶ 31 You are going to hear about an unusual eating experience. First, circle the option you think is correct. Then listen and check.

1 Darwin is in the *north / south* of Australia.
2 The native people of Australia are known as *Aboriginal people / Maori.*
3 The native people of Australia are known for *collecting / growing* their food.

5 ▶ 31 Listen again. Check (✓) the things the speaker ate.

ants	crocodile eggs	crocodile meat	leaves
lemons	trees	water lilies	grass

the Outback (n) /ði'autbæk/ the desert areas of Australia where few people live
watering hole (n) /'wɔːtr'ɪŋ həʊl/ a small pool of water where animals go to drink

6 Which sentence (a–c) best reflects the speaker's opinion?

a Bush tucker only gives you part of the food you need.

b The things you can eat in the Outback are nutritious but taste horrible.

c It's not very hard to find food in the Outback if you know where to look.

Grammar modal verbs (1)

7 Rewrite the visitor information from a national park with modal verbs. Sometimes more than one answer is possible.

> **1** Camping in the park is not allowed.
> **2** Picnics are restricted to designated areas.
> **3** Do not swim in the river.
> **4** It's a good idea to carry water with you.
> **5** It's not necessary to show identification to enter.
> **6** Approaching wild animals is not advisable.
> **7** Report any incidents with wild animals.

1 _____
2 _____
3 _____
4 _____
5 _____
6 _____
7 _____

8 Pronunciation weak forms

▶ **32** Listen and repeat the sentences. Pay attention to how *to* is not stressed.

9 Grammar extra past modal verbs

▶ PAST MODAL VERBS	
Modal verbs that express obligation, permission, and ability have the following past forms:	
obligation	
have/has to	*had to, didn't have to*
permission	
is/are allowed to	*was/were allowed to, wasn't/ weren't allowed to*
ability	
can	*could, couldn't*

Complete the paragraph about a school trip with the correct past modal verbs in parentheses.

When I was in middle school, we went on a school trip to the mountains. We went by bus and then walked for about a mile. We [1] _____ (have to / carry) our own backpacks, and mine was really heavy. I remember that everyone [2] _____ (have to / wear) orange hats when we were traveling, and nobody wanted to. We did lots of outdoor activities like climbing and stuff, but we [3] _____ (not allowed / go) into the woods alone. We [4] _____ (have to / stay) in pairs. We learned how to make a campfire, but I [5] _____ (can / do) that already because my mom had taught me. We cooked and ate outside, but we [6] _____ (not have to / sleep) outside—there were cabins with six beds in each one. It rained for the last three days, so we [7] _____ (allowed / eat) in the cabins, and on the last day we got takeout from a nearby cafe.

5b Strategies for success

Reading willpower

1 Read the article on page 39 and answer the quiz questions.

2 Read the article again and find words that mean:

1 an objective, an aim (n): _____

2 people (n): _____

3 decisions or promises you make to yourself (n): _____

4 courageous, without fear (adj): _____

5 tests of your abilities (n): _____

6 a starting point or basis for something (n): _____

3 Match these missing sentences with the three quotes at the end of the article.

1 If you don't take a risk, you won't know what you're capable of.

2 You can develop your willpower if you want to.

3 If you give up, everyone will give up.

Grammar first conditional; when, as soon as, unless, until, before

4 Write full sentences with the simple present and *will* + infinitive.

1 you eat a healthy meal / feel better afterward

_____

_____

2 I watch a movie / enjoy myself

_____

_____

3 you find a new route to work / save money

_____

_____

4 you take chewing gum with you / not need to smoke

_____

_____

5 you not buy chocolate / not eat it

_____

_____

6 you live longer / have a good diet

_____

_____

5 Rewrite the sentences with the word in parentheses without changing the meaning.

1 You won't achieve anything if you don't take risks.
(unless)

_____

2 Your friends will help you if you ask them.
(as soon as)

_____

3 You'll be successful if you plan things carefully.
(when)

_____

4 You won't know what you can do if you don't try.
(until)

_____

5 You'll make a lot of mistakes and then you'll succeed.
(before)

_____

Vocabulary a healthy lifestyle

6 Which of these strategies are not part of a healthy lifestyle?

changing bad habits
cutting down on relaxation
avoiding outdoor activities
giving up junk food
taking up smoking
cutting out fatty food

7 Dictation healthy living

 **33** Listen and write the parts of the sentences. Then match the beginnings (1–4) with the endings (a–d) to make logical sentences.

1 _____ ___

2 _____ ___

3 _____ ___

4 _____ ___

a _____

b _____

c _____

d _____

Strategies for success

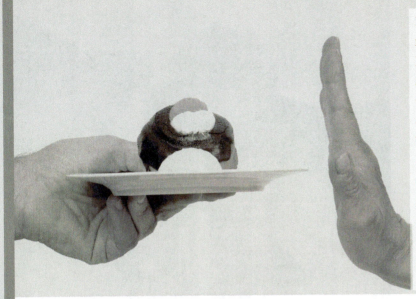

Every month you pay a large sum of money for your gym membership. But some months you don't even go. Sound familiar? What does it take to achieve a goal? Why do some determined individuals pull their boots on and achieve what few would even dare to try? Find out the secrets of three successful adventurers below. But first, imagine you want to make some changes in your life: do our quiz and check out how much willpower you have.

1 You get home after a long day at work. What do you do for your evening meal?
a   make a healthy meal using fresh ingredients
b   call for a delivery of fast food
c   heat up a frozen dinner

2 Summer is coming, and you want to look your best. You have a free evening ahead. Do you … ?
a   go out jogging
b   read a magazine about healthy living
c   watch a movie

3 You've been spending too much money recently. Your route to work takes you through a shopping mall. Do you … ?
a   find a different route that avoids stores
b   take the usual route and buy yourself something nice
c   take the usual route but not spend any money

4 You decided to quit smoking a while ago. You're going out with friends. Do you … ?
a   take some chewing gum with you
b   leave your cigarettes at home
c   take three cigarettes with you

If your answers are mostly **a**, you'll probably stick to your resolutions. If your answers are mostly **c**, you have the will but perhaps not enough power. If your answers are mostly **b**, you'd better read what the experts say. You don't have to be an intrepid adventurer to find these comments useful. We're all faced with challenges, big and small, in our everyday lives.

Mental challenges are as difficult to pass as endurance tests. You pass through failure to success. You do not avoid failure. To me, the most exciting time is when things aren't going right. As a leader, you can't give up. _____
Robert D. Ballard, marine explorer

When I had to decide between the comfort of a staff news job and the risk of freelance photography, my mother told me that no great chasm was ever leaped in two small jumps. _____
Jodi Cobb, National Geographic *photographer*

People can build their willpower deliberately. We are born with a certain amount, but that is just a platform. I think you can build willpower and be strong and achieve a lot. Start with a step you feel comfortable with and take it one step ahead. _____
Børge Ousland, polar explorer

> **dare** (v) /dɛr/ be brave enough to do something
> **endurance** (n) /ɪnˈdjʊərns/ the ability to keep doing something difficult, unpleasant, or painful for a long time
> **chasm** (n) /ˈkæzm/ a long deep narrow hole in ice or rock

5c Alternative lifestyles

Vocabulary **modern life**

1 Circle the correct option to make things associated with a 24-hour society.

1 *electric / natural* light
2 *high / low* blood pressure
3 *outdoor / indoor* jobs
4 *day / night* work schedules
5 *irregular / regular* sleep

Listening **alternative lifestyles**

2 ▶ 34 Listen to a radio program and circle the correct option (a–c).

1 Lisa Napoli went to _____ .
  a Nepal
  b Tibet
  c Bhutan

2 She went there to _____ .
  a work
  b visit friends
  c go backpacking

3 As a result of her experience, she _____ .
  a became rich
  b learned to be content
  c gave up her job

4 Mark Boyle _____ .
  a changed his job
  b stayed in his local environment
  c tried to live in a new culture

5 He decided to give up _____ .
  a eating meat
  b all his possessions
  c using money

6 He learned the importance of _____ .
  a work
  b people
  c possessions

3 Which statement(s) (a–c) agree(s) with what the host said?

a Both Napoli and Boyle found they were happier with fewer material things.
b Neither Napoli nor Boyle was able to give up the 24-hour lifestyle.
c Napoli and Boyle's experiences are not applicable to anyone else.

Word focus *so*

4 Match the beginnings of the sentences (1–6) with the endings (a–f).

1 I didn't know it was so easy ____
2 Please let me know if you're coming so ____
3 Thanks so much ____
4 There are ten of us, so ____
5 Tim shouldn't get so angry ____
6 We've started going to the gym, and so far ____

a for your help with my shopping yesterday.
b I can reserve a table.
c this month we've been six times.
d to make cake!
e we'll need a large table.
f with other drivers—there's no point.

5d Eating out

Vocabulary restaurants

1 Put the restaurant customer's words in order to make statements and questions.

1 of / that / made / what's

   _____ ?

2 taste / they / like / what / do

   _____ ?

3 I'll / think / that / try / I

   _____ .

4 come / does / with / vegetables / it

   _____ ?

5 the / have / same / I'll

   _____ .

2 Grammar extra *need to*

> ▶ **NEED TO**
>
> We can use *need to* to say that it's important or necessary, rather than obligatory, to do something.
>   *Is that restaurant busy at lunchtime? Do we need to reserve a table?*
>
> We can use *need to* when *have to* or *must* would sound too strong.
>
> *Don't need to* is the same as *don't have to*. They both mean that it's not necessary to do something, or that you can choose not to do it.
>   *You don't need to have an appetizer if you don't want one.* (also *You don't have to have an appetizer …*)

Complete the sentences with *need to* or *have to*.

1 Do we _____ wait for the waiter to show us our table? (necessary)

2 You _____ dress up—it's a pretty casual place. (not necessary)

3 It's kind of formal—you _____ wear a jacket and tie. (obligatory)

4 They don't accept advance reservations. You _____ stand in line if it's busy. (obligatory)

Real life describing dishes

3 Which is the odd word out in the sentences describing dishes?

1 It's a little like *potatoes / lamb / baked.*

2 They taste *salty / fish / spicy.*

3 It's made from *meat / vegetables / hot.*

4 It's a kind of *bland / boiled / fried* dish.

4 Read the comments. Is the person describing an appetizer (A), main course (M), or dessert (D)?

1 It's made of milk and it's really sweet. It's usually served cold. ____

2 They're sort of little packets of vegetables. They're pretty spicy. ____

3 It's a baked dish made from different kinds of meat and vegetables, with rice or pasta. ____

4 It tastes a little salty. It's a sort of spread for bread or toast. ____

5 Pronunciation disappearing sounds

a ▶ 35 Listen to the sentences with these words. Cross out the part of the word which is not pronounced—the disappearing sound—in each word. Then listen again and repeat the sentences.

1 comfortable   3 national

2 evening   4 traveling

b ▶ 36 How do you pronounce these words from the Student Book? Listen and repeat.

| camera | poisoning | several | snorkeling |

6 Listen and respond talking to a waiter

▶ 37 Listen to the waiter's questions. Respond with your own words. Then compare your response with the model answer that follows.

> *Are you ready to order?*

> *Not quite. We just need a minute.*

5e We look forward to your reply

Writing a formal letter

1 Writing skill explaining consequences

a Your local fitness center was refurbished recently, and, as part of this process, there have been other changes. Look at the notes and write these headings in the correct spaces (1–3).

| cafeteria | opening times | prices |

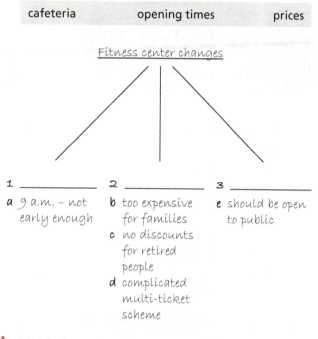

Fitness center changes

1 _____ 2 _____ 3 _____

a 9 a.m. – not early enough

b too expensive for families

c no discounts for retired people

d complicated multi-ticket scheme

e should be open to public

b Match the parts of the sentences. Then complete the sentences using these expressions for explaining consequences.

| Consequently Therefore | has led to will result in | means that |

1 The swimming pool doesn't open until 9 a.m.
_____

2 Taking away discounts for retired people
_____

3 The multi-ticket scheme is too complicated.
_____

4 Opening the cafeteria to the public _____
_____

5 The price increase _____
_____

a fewer students using the center.
b people don't take advantage of offers.
c people can't swim before they go to work.
d they can't afford to use the center very often.
e more people using the center.

2 Use the information from Exercise 1b to complete this letter. Refer to Student's Book and Workbook Unit 4 to review formal style.

Dear Sir,

We are writing to express our concern at the recent changes to Newton Community Fitness Center. We are concerned about _____
_____
_____

In our view, _____
_____
_____
_____
_____

We also note that _____
_____
_____

In addition, _____
_____
_____

Finally, we feel that _____
_____
_____

We request that you review these changes to the services that the fitness center provides to its users.

Yours sincerely,

Singh

PH Singh
Newton Students' Association

Wordbuilding
phrasal verbs

> ▶ **WORDBUILDING** phrasal verbs
>
> Phrasal verbs with *down* and *up* often describe change.
> *cut down, give up*

1 Complete the sentences with the correct form of these verbs and *up*.

go	grow	put
take	speed	

1 The prices in the café have _____ since we were last here.

2 They've _____ some abstract paintings. It looks really different now.

3 I think I'll _____ cooking this winter.

4 If this bus doesn't _____ a little, we'll be late.

5 You need to _____ . Stop behaving like a child.

2 Complete the sentences with the correct form of these verbs and *down*.

bring	come	get
take	slow	

1 Strawberries are expensive now, but the price will _____ soon.

2 I'm on a diet because I have to _____ my weight _____ .

3 You'll have an accident unless you _____ .

4 We can't _____ these warning notices _____ — they have to be visible.

5 There's a danger that the protests will _____ the government.

Learning skills planning writing

3 Look at the list of strategies for planning writing. Which strategies has this student used?

- noting down the questions your writing needs to answer
- noting down the purpose of your written text
- thinking about who the reader is
- brainstorming ideas
- brainstorming useful vocabulary
- using a mind map to organize words
- organizing words in a table
- following a model text
- listing useful expressions
- listing useful linking words
- writing notes and short sentences
- organizing sentences by sequence or idea
- writing the same idea in different ways

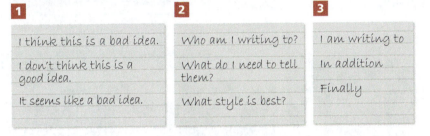

1
I think this is a bad idea.
I don't think this is a good idea.
It seems like a bad idea.

2
Who am I writing to?
What do I need to tell them?
What style is best?

3
I am writing to
In addition
Finally

4 Answer the questions with reference to the writing you have done for the writing tasks in Student's Book and Workbook Units 1–5.

1 Which of the strategies did you use?
_____

2 How helpful did you find them?
_____

3 Which is the most useful strategy for you? Why?
_____

Check!

5 Complete the crossword with the answers to the clues. All these words are in Student's Book Unit 5.

Across

2 A savory banana

5 A dangerous fish to eat

6 Try _____ fish and ackee in Jamaica

Down

1 Something in food and drink that increased blood pressure

2 _____ Napoletana

3 Order this before your main course

4 Potato chips, candy, chocolate, etc.

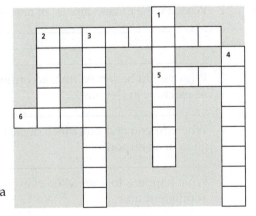

Unit 6 Mysteries

6a Join the line

Listening lining up

One gold double serum.
Twice the anti-ageing power.

双萃赋活精华露
Double Serum

1 You are going to listen to an excerpt from a radio program about lining up. Look at the photo. What do you think the people are lining up for?

2 ▶ 38 Listen to the excerpt. Answer the questions.

1 What three things does the host say are typically American?
_____
_____
_____

2 What are the three examples of lines she gives?
_____
_____
_____

3 Who should be served first, according to researchers in Denmark?
_____

4 When do you find out which departure gate to go to in an airport?
_____

5 What happens to lines when everyone arrives at different times?
_____

6 Does the system described by the researchers work all the time?
_____

3 ▶ 38 Listen again. Complete the sentences.

1 You don't find lining up in every _____ .

2 The problem with traditional lines is that people tend to _____ too early.

3 People _____ differently if this system is used.

4 The really important point here is that you have to know in _____ that this is the system.

Word focus *long*

4 Complete the sentences with these expressions.

all night long	as long as	long
long enough	long time	too long

1 Everyone has to wait a _____ .

2 I don't usually ride the bus to work because it takes _____ .

3 You can borrow my bike _____ you bring it back on Monday.

4 I'm worried about the baby. She was crying _____ .

5 My essay wasn't _____ because I only wrote 200 words.

6 Will you be _____ at the mall? Because we have a lot to do at home.

Grammar purpose: *to*, *for*, and *so that*

5 Complete the sentences with *to*, *for*, or *so that*.

1 I always arrive early _____ I'm first in line.
2 The GPS is great _____ finding the route to new places.
3 My friend was in the hospital _____ an operation last week.
4 My sisters and I had to wait a long time _____ the bus.
5 The bank called _____ tell me my new card was ready.
6 I learned to drive _____ I could look for a better job.
7 There are lots of signs in the city _____ tell you where interesting buildings are.
8 We should get together _____ dinner next week.

6 Match the questions (1–6) with the answers (a–f). Then write answers with *to*, *so that*, and *for*. You can change the verb form and/or add more words. There is more than one possibility in each case.

1 Why did you decide to take the exam? ____
2 Why has Rich gone to town today? ____
3 What's that new machine in your kitchen? ____
4 Why are you waiting here? ____
5 Why are you in a hurry? ____
6 What's "Fit-trak"? ____

a get home before it rains.
b improve my resume.
c make vegetable and fruit juice.
d (pick up) the tickets for his vacation.
e (see) the cycle race when it goes by.
f an app—counts how far you walk.

1 _____
2 _____
3 _____
4 _____
5 _____
6 _____

7 Grammar extra *as if / as though / like*

> **AS IF / AS THOUGH / LIKE**
>
> *The sky is black. It looks as if / as though / like it's going to rain.*
> *Jack is late today. It looks as if / as though / like he's not coming.*
> *Why is David shouting? He sounds as if / as though / like he's about to explode.*

Match the sentences (1–8) with the phrases (a–h). Then write complete sentences with *look / sound* and *as if / as though / like*.

1 Let's go to the beach tomorrow. ____
   _____
2 This line is really long. ____
   _____
3 Why is the car making that noise? ____
   _____
4 Why are you so red? ____
   _____
5 Paco is very happy today. ____
   _____
6 Jenna and Tara have already left the office. ____
   _____
7 Susan said she's busy on Sunday. ____
   _____
8 Your vacation photos are great. ____
   _____

a A part is falling off.
b He had a nice weekend.
c It's going to be sunny.
d She's not coming to lunch.
e They've finished their work.
f We'll be here for hours.
g You had a good time.
h You've been for a run.

6b Easter Island

Reading Mysterious statues

1 Look at the pictures and read the captions to find out what *moai* and *pukao* are.

2 Read the article and answer the questions.

1 How close is Easter Island to South America?
_____

2 How many *moai* are on the island?
_____

3 What are the *moai* made of?
_____

4 How old is the youngest *moai*?
_____

5 Do all of the *moai* have hats?
_____

6 Are the *moai* and the hats made from the same material?
_____

3 Read the article again. Are the sentences true (T) or false (F)?

1	The statues were not made on Easter Island.	T	F
2	The statues must have been moved from their original location.	T	F
3	The red *pukao* could have had a special meaning.	T	F
4	The red *pukao* must have been made before the statues.	T	F
5	The statues might have been moved with ropes.	T	F

Easter Island statues, or *moai*. The second figure from the right wears a *pukao*.

Mysterious statues

Easter Island, or Rapa Nui, is one of the world's most remote inhabited islands. It's part of the Polynesian islands in the South Pacific Ocean, and it is 2,000 kilometers away from the nearest inhabited island (Pitcairn Island) and 3,000 kilometers from the coast of Chile. The mystery of Easter Island is not really how people arrived there, but it is connected to what those people did—they made huge stone statues. The statues are so big that nobody knows exactly how they were moved and placed into the positions we see them in today.

There are more than 800 of these giant human figures, called *moai*, at various sites around the island. The statues are carved out of volcanic stone, and they represent the islanders' ancestors. Scientific techniques like carbon dating suggest that the *moai* were carved over a very long period, perhaps about 600 years. The last statues were probably made about 400 years ago. Some of the *moai* are wearing "hats"—these are round red stone additions to the top of the statues. These hats, called *pukao*, are over two meters high. It seems probable that the meaning of the *pukao* was connected to how important the ancestors were. In other words, the figures with *pukao* might have been especially important people.

Most of the statues are made from stone. This stone is located far from where the statues stand today. In addition, the *pukao* are made from a different type of rock to the main statue, which means they must have been added after the main figure was carved. Carl Lipo, an archeologist from California State University, believes the Polynesians rolled the *pukao* along the ground and up ramps eight meters high to the top of the statues. He also believes the islanders were incredible engineers and were able to move heavy objects using ropes and only a few men. So far, however, nobody has shown for certain that either of these systems work.

carbon dating (n) /ˈkɑrbən deɪtɪŋ/ a method for finding out the age of old objects
ramp (n) /ræmp/ a slope that connects things which are at different levels

Grammar certainty and possibility

4 Circle the correct option.

1 The Easter Island statues are huge. You *can't / must* feel small when you stand next to them.

2 It's a national holiday today. Car trips *could / must* take a little longer.

3 There's only one boat here today. The others *may not / must* be out to sea.

4 Our flight is at six and it's only four o'clock now, so we *can't / might* be too late.

5 The weather forecast was for rain, but I suppose it *could / can't* be wrong.

6 Francis wasn't on that bus, so he *can't / must* be coming on a different one.

5 Complete the conversation with the words.

can't have been	may have seen	must have been

A: This looks interesting—I like documentaries about people in history.

B: Yes, it's just started. It looks really familiar, though. I think I ¹ _____ it before.

A: Really? It says in the paper that it's a new program, so it ² _____ on before.

B: Really? It ³ _____ a trailer then. I know it was advertised a lot.

***Pukao* can be up to 2.5 meters high.**

Easter Island is part of Polynesia and is a UNESCO World Heritage Site.

6 Complete the conversation with the words.

can't have been	might have been
could have called	must have been
might have been	must have had

A: That's weird. I have four missed calls on my phone.

B: Same number each time? It ¹ _____ important if the same person called four times.

A: No, different numbers. But they didn't leave any messages, so it ² _____ very important. I wonder how I missed them?

B: You ³ _____ your phone switched off.

A: No, I didn't.

B: Well, you ⁴ _____ busy or the volume ⁵ _____ turned down or something.

A: Yes, maybe. Well, I don't recognize the numbers, so I suppose the people ⁶ _____ by mistake.

7 Pronunciation weak form of *have*

▶ 39 Listen and repeat five of the sentences from Exercises 5 and 6.

8 Dictation speculating

▶ 40 Listen and write the comments you hear. Then match them with the situations (a–e).

1 _____
_____ ___

2 _____
_____ ___

3 _____
_____ ___

4 _____
_____ ___

5 _____
_____ ___

a You can't get through to your friend's cell phone.

b Your friends haven't arrived for your birthday party.

c Your sister's gone out. Her keys are on the table.

d The TV show you are watching seems familiar.

e Your boss is very late for a meeting.

6c Crop circles

Reading and listening
crop circles

1 a crop circle

2 a wallaby

3 a poppy

4 poppy-seed capsules

1 ▶ 41 Listen to a news story from Australia. What's the connection between the photos?

2 ▶ 41 Read the news story. Complete the article with these words. You can use the words as many times as you think necessary. Then listen again and check.

extraterrestrial	hoaxers	humans	patterns
physical	poppies	tools	wallabies

3 Read these comments that people made after hearing this news story. Which comments are supported by the information given in the story?

a "Crop circles must be hoaxes because there is no other rational explanation."
b "Wallabies live in Australia, so they can't have made the U.K. crop circles."
c "I think the crop circles might have been the result of animal activity."

4 All these words are in the news story. Which groups of words (a–c) can replace the words in bold in these sentences?

a	b	c
circular	explanation	bizarre
complex	suggestion	odd
geometric	view	weird

1 That's an interesting **theory**. ____
2 I've read about this **strange** phenomenon. ____
3 The building has an **intricate** shape. ____

A bizarre theory

The strange and fascinating phenomenon of crop circles—which actually aren't simply circular but form intricate geometric [1] _patterns_ in farm fields—has inspired many possible explanations over the years. Crop-circle enthusiasts who prefer paranormal explanations for the circles believe that they must be messages left behind by [2] _____ visitors, while more conventionally scientific-minded people have theorized that they might have resulted from natural [3] _____ forces, such as wind or heat. But now, there's another, even more bizarre explanation: [4] _____ .

As BBC News and many other news outlets are reporting, Lara Giddings, Attorney General for the Australian state of Tasmania, told a Parliamentary hearing that [5] _____ have been eating [6] _____ in fields that provide legal opium for morphine and other painkillers. Apparently, according to Giddings, the [7] _____ are eating the [8] _____ and then becoming so disoriented that they run around in the fields erratically, creating paths that resemble crop circles.

An official with an Australian poppy-cultivation company told ABC News that in the process of consuming the poppy-seed capsules, the [9] _____ often also eat some of the substances that cause opium's hallucinogenic effect in [10] _____ . The weird suggestion that animals may have been the cause of Australian crop circles, however, doesn't really explain the crop-circle phenomenon. Are they capable of creating the sort of intricate geometric [11] _____ seen in most crop circles? What about the crop circles found thousands of kilometers away from Australia, in the U.K.?

This odd explanation also doesn't account for the alternative view that crop circles are nothing more than elaborate jokes. A University of Oregon physicist, Richard Taylor, speculates that crop-circle [12] _____ may now be using increasingly sophisticated [13] _____ such as GPS devices and laser pointers to burn complex [14] _____ into fields.

6d You must be joking!

Real life reacting to surprising news

1 Read the news stories. Do you think they are true or false?

1 More than a dozen scientists and yeti enthusiasts from Canada, Estonia, Sweden, and the U.S. flew to Siberia yesterday to exchange findings with their Russian counterparts at a day-long yeti conference.

2 One of the U.K.'s most famous poets has written a book of poems about bees.

3 Representatives of the fishing industry warn that tuna is almost extinct.

4 The U.K. government has announced a new initiative to use the decimal system. From April 1 there will be ten hours in each day.

2 Complete the expressions for showing surprise with these words.

joking	kidding	mistake	off	right	sure

1 Come _____ it!
2 That can't be _____ !
3 They must have made a _____ .
4 You must be _____ !
5 You're _____ me!
6 Are you _____ ?

3 Pronunciation showing interest and disbelief

▶ 42 Listen and repeat the expressions from Exercise 2. Pay attention to your intonation.

4 Listen and respond reacting to surprising news

▶ 43 Listen to the statements. Imagine a friend of yours is speaking. Respond with your own words. Then compare your response with the model answer that follows.

Look! It's snowing outside.

Are you sure?

6e In the news

Writing a news story

1 Writing skill structuring a news story

a Read the mixed-up notes (a–d) of a news story. Which section is the introductory sentence? _____

> **a** The area _____ (be) temporarily affected as the lightning _____ (cut off) electricity. Later, firefighters _____ (say) the man was incredibly lucky.
>
> **b** The fire department _____ (respond) immediately to the call. According to the owner of the house, it all _____ (happen) extremely quickly.
>
> **c** An unbelievable three bolts of lightning _____ (strike) a house last night, but fortunately, nobody was hurt.
>
> **d** Neighbors _____ (call) the fire department after the first bolt of lightning _____ (start) a small fire.

b Write the story in the correct sequence and with the correct verb forms.

_____
_____
_____
_____
_____
_____

Vocabulary -ly adverbs in stories

2 Write the six -ly adverbs in the story next to the adverbs with similar meanings.

1 briefly: _____
2 instantly: _____
3 luckily: _____
4 very: _____
5 rapidly: _____
6 unbelievably: _____

3 Complete the sentences using the adverbs you used in Exercise 2.

1 She spoke _____ slowly, but I still didn't understand.
2 _____ , it wasn't serious.
3 I only worked there _____ .
4 It was _____ dangerous.
5 She replied to my email _____ .
6 The fire was _____ put out.

4 Grammar extra -ly adverbs

> **▶ -LY ADVERBS**
>
> We use -ly adverbs with:
> **1 main verbs**
> *The fire department responded immediately to the call.*
> **2 whole sentences or clauses**
> *Fortunately, nobody was hurt.*
> **3 adjectives**
> *The man was incredibly lucky.*
> **4 past participles of verbs**
> *The area was temporarily affected.*
> **5 other adverbs**
> *It all happened extremely quickly.*

Rewrite the sentences with the adverbs in parentheses in the correct position. Make changes to punctuation as necessary.

1 nobody knows what happened (incredibly)
_____

2 this is not the first time this has happened (sadly)
_____

3 the man spoke about the incident (sadly)
_____

4 things are returning to normal (gradually)
_____

5 we were shocked by the news (incredibly)
_____

Wordbuilding nouns and verbs

> **WORDBUILDING nouns and verbs**
>
> Some nouns and verbs have the same form. The meanings of the two forms can have similar (e.g., *land*) or unconnected (e.g., *book*) meanings.

1 Each word below has a verb and a noun form. Say if the verb form is regular (R) or irregular (I), and if the noun form is countable (C) or uncountable (U).

1 call	_R, C_	8 heat	_____
2 cause	_____	9 match	_____
3 cook	_____	10 paint	_____
4 email	_____	11 phone	_____
5 fall	_____	12 shop	_____
6 farm	_____	13 show	_____
7 fire	_____	14 stop	_____

2 Complete the pairs of sentences with a word from Exercise 1. Use the correct verb and noun forms.

1 a Everyone should learn how to _____ a few basic dishes.
  b My aunt is a _____ in the local school kitchen.
2 a Police are not yet sure what _____ the accident.
  b Eating too much junk food is a major _____ of poor health.
3 a What's happening? Why has the line _____ moving?
  b The express bus is quicker because there aren't any _____ between here and Chicago.
4 a Can you _____ me the details of your trip?
  b I didn't get the _____ about the new timetable.
5 a Have you decided what to _____ your new puppy?
  b I'll give you a _____ when my plane lands.
6 a The forest _____ was started by a lightning strike.
  b The company will _____ any employee who is regularly late for work.
7 a There was a big _____ in the number of visitors to Toronto last year.
  b I don't like climbing because I always think I'm going to _____ .

Learning skills using the internet (1)

Listening to the news on the internet is one of the best ways of getting additional listening practice.

3 Here are some reasons why listening to the news is often easier than listening to other things. Match the beginnings of the sentences (1–4) with the endings (a–d).

1 News stories are often international, so ____
2 News stories tend to follow a similar format, so ____
3 News items are often narratives, which ____
4 News videos give you pictures ____

a to support the story you are listening to.
b you might have already heard some information in your own language.
c tend to be easier to understand than opinion items.
d you can concentrate more on the actual language of the story.

4 You can use the same set of questions to help you understand any news story better. Can you complete these questions?

1 Where _____ ?
2 When _____ ?
3 Who _____ ?
4 What _____ ?
5 How _____ ?
6 Why _____ ?

5 ▶ 44 Listen to two stories from different news websites. Take notes using the questions from Exercise 4.

Check!

6 Find the four places in these anagrams and write them in the correct spaces (1–4). The letters in the shaded squares spell the name of a country in South America.

1 aeilnopsy   3 adeknmr
2 cehil   4 aaailrstu

1								A
2	H							
3			M					
4	A							

51

Unit 7 Living space

7a In the past

Vocabulary in the city

1 Complete the comments about New York that tourists left on a website. There is one extra word.

atmosphere	blocks	built-up	financial	residents
skyscrapers	neighborhoods		public transportation	

1 Our hotel was only two _____ away from Central Park.
2 The city's _____ seem to come from every country in the world.
3 _____ was cheap compared to taxis.
4 The _____ at night on Broadway is magical.
5 The famous _____ don't disappoint you—they seem to touch the clouds.
6 We had a great time visiting Wall Street and the _____ district.
7 I enjoyed spending time in Central Park to get away from the _____ areas.

Grammar *used to, would,* and the simple past

2 Circle the sentences where *used to* can replace the simple past.

1 This area didn't have so many skyscrapers before.
2 The pollution here was much worse than it is now.
3 The local residents campaigned for better public transportation.
4 The atmosphere wasn't so relaxed in the past.
5 There weren't as many crowded neighborhoods.

3 Rewrite the sentences you checked in Exercise 2 with *used to* or *didn't use to.*

_____
_____
_____
_____

4 Circle the sentences where *would* can replace *used to.*

1 When I was young, we used to live next to my school.
2 My friends and I used to play in the street.
3 There used to be a lot of traffic along this road.
4 I didn't use to like my neighbors.
5 We didn't use to go out if it was raining.

5 Rewrite the sentences from Exercise 4 with *would* where possible. Rewrite the other sentences with the simple past.

1 _____
2 _____
3 _____
4 _____
5 _____

6 Dictation childhood

▶ 45 Listen and write the sentences. Then write your own answers for the three questions.

1 _____
2 Q: _____
   A: _____
3 _____
4 Q: _____
   A: _____
5 _____
6 Q: _____
   A: _____

Listening Timbuktu

7 ▶ **46** Listen to a podcast about Timbuktu. Are these facts true (T) or false (F)?

Timbuktu used to be:

1	an important Islamic city.	T	F
2	a World Heritage Site.	T	F
3	a major trading center.	T	F
4	a destination for religious scholars.	T	F
5	invaded regularly by Moroccan forces.	T	F

8 ▶ **46** Listen again. Complete the sentences.

1 Timbuktu used to be a place of _____ .
2 Timbuktu has a great _____ of ancient manuscripts.
3 The city's _____ was important in its history.
4 Timbuktu is on the Niger _____ .
5 _____ trains used to pass through the city.
6 The river brought cargoes of _____ and slaves to the city.
7 After the 16th century, the _____ began to leave Timbuktu.

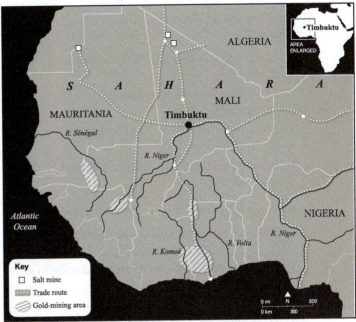

scholar (n) /ˈskɑlər/ an academic or specialist in a subject
cargoes (n) /ˈkɑrgoʊz/ products being taken from one place to another on ships and aircraft

7b Changing places

Reading an ecovillage

1 Read the article. Are the sentences true (T) or false (F)?

1 Matavenero is one of 2,000 ecovillages in Spain.　　T　F

2 The village is an international community.　　T　F

3 It's a three-hour drive to Matavenero from the nearest town.　　T　F

4 Life in the village is easier than typical modern life.　　T　F

2 Read the article again and answer the questions.

1 Why are the rural villages in Spain abandoned?
_____

2 Why did the five German people decide to go to Matavenero?
_____

3 What other reasons do people have for moving to Matavenero?
_____
_____

4 What activities do the people in the village do?
_____
_____

Grammar comparison: adverbs

3 Rewrite the sentences using the word in parentheses. Begin with the word in bold.

1 Sandra doesn't work as hard as **Toni.** (harder)
_____

2 I don't cook as well as **my parents.** (better)
_____

3 **Toni** drives less carefully than Sandra. (as)
_____

4 Brian passed his exams more easily than **Andrew.** (as)
_____

5 My sister doesn't speak English as badly as **my brother.** (worse)
_____

6 Usain Bolt can run faster than **most people.** (as)
_____

Grammar comparison: patterns

4 Complete the comments using the words in parentheses to make comparative patterns.

1 I don't spend a lot of time in the house because I get bored. I like to be outdoors and active. In fact, _____ (active I am / happy I am).

2 I live alone, but I like inviting people to my apartment—I always prepare lunch on Sunday for friends. The lunch party _____ (get big / big) because my friends always want to bring more friends.

3 I hate doing housework, and so these days I do it _____ (more quickly). I have so many things I'd rather do!

4 Apartment-sharing is OK, but the _____ (big apartment / good it is). If everyone has some space, there aren't as many arguments.

5 I've been studying a lot recently, and so my room _____ (get messy / messy). I can't clean it up until after my exams.

6 People are living _____ (far / far) away from cities these days. I think it's a good idea.

5 Pronunciation extra and

▶ 47 Listen and repeat the sentences with comparative patterns. Notice how *and* is not stressed and sounds like *n.*

1 I'm getting faster and faster at this game.

2 We come to this café more and more often.

3 Phones are getting less and less expensive.

4 People are traveling farther and farther from home these days.

5 The old town's streets became emptier and emptier.

6 Life in the village got harder and harder.

An ecovillage

In rural Spain, there are more than 2,000 villages that used to be full of life but are now abandoned. Their residents left to move to cities or to other countries, and slowly the villages became emptier and emptier until there was nobody left. Now, however, some of these remote places are coming to life again as "ecovillages." Their new residents are looking for a simpler way of life.

The little village of Matavenero, in northern Spain, is one example. In 1989, five friends from Germany were looking for a place where they could have a better life than in their large German city. They heard about Matavenero. Getting permission from the local government much more quickly than they expected, they moved there to start a new life. A few more people from Denmark joined them, and they began to build the ecovillage that exists today. Everyone has their own reasons for moving to Matavenero. Some wanted to live more peacefully, some more cheaply or less stressfully. But most of the residents seem to feel that the simpler the life, the better.

As there is no road to the village, you can't get there by car. It takes about three hours to walk there from the nearest road. Once there, you won't find many of the typical things that make up modern life, although there is a small school, a bakery, a library, and a small store. The Matavenero residents grow food, make things to sell locally, and some also work in regular jobs. This kind of life is attractive to lots of people and some come to try it out. However, some of the new arrivals find that they have to work harder than they expected, and more than half actually leave before a year. But for the rest of the community, the village is a successful way of life.

7c Megacities

Listening 19.20.21

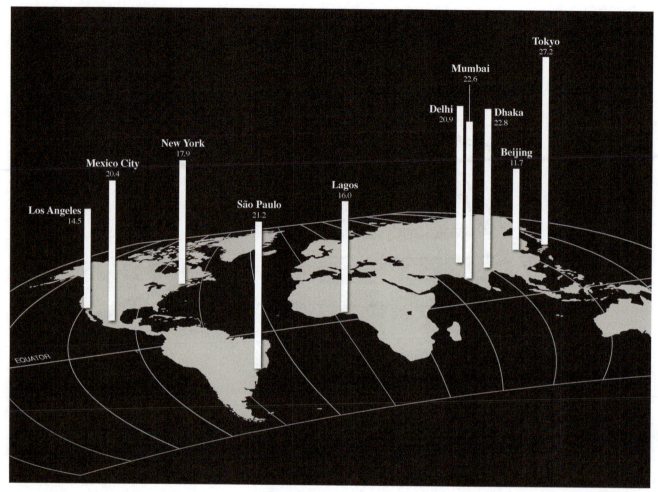

Population in millions

1 Can you name the five biggest cities in the world? Look at the map and check your ideas.

2 ▶ 48 You are going to listen to a podcast about a project called 19.20.21 by architect Richard Saul Wurman. What do you think the name 19.20.21 means? Listen and check your answer.

3 ▶ 48 Listen again. Circle the correct answers. More than one may be correct.

1 Why did Wurman begin the 19.20.21 project?
   a because cities are getting bigger and bigger
   b to understand more about the move to urban life
   c because he couldn't find enough information about cities

2 Why do people keep moving to cities?
   a to get better opportunities
   b because important institutions are there
   c because they have no choice

3 Why is a project like this needed?
   a so we can compare one city with another
   b so we understand cities and can improve them more successfully
   c because we don't know how to improve our cities

4 Complete the sentences with four of these places.

Beijing	Lagos	Los Angeles	Mumbai	Tokyo

1 The biggest city in the world today is
   _____ .

2 _____ is the fastest growing city.

3 The most densely populated city is
   _____ .

4 _____ covers the largest area.

7d To rent or to buy?

Real life expressing preferences

1 Grammar extra *prefer* and *would rather*

▶ **PREFER and WOULD RATHER**

I prefer	+	verb + *-ing* noun infinitive
I'd prefer		noun infinitive
I'd rather		base form

We use the simple present form *prefer* to talk about things in general. We use the conditional form of *prefer* and *would rather* to talk about the future or a hypothetical situation.

Look at the grammar box. Then complete the sentences.

1 A: There's a nice apartment for sale on my block if you're interested.
  B: Well, I'd rather _____ (rent) somewhere before I buy.

2 A: What are you looking for? One or two bedrooms?
  B: I'd prefer _____ (have) an extra room, so two.

3 A: Do you usually take the bus to work?
  B: No. I prefer _____ (walk), especially when the weather is good.

4 A: Have you made your mind up about going out tonight?
  B: Yes. I'd prefer _____ (stay) in.

5 I _____ (prefer) action movies to romances.

6 Do you prefer _____ (watch) TV or _____ (read) in the evenings?

7 A: Do you want a cup of tea?
  B: I'd rather _____ (have) coffee, actually.

2 Match the preferences (1–8) with the reasons (a–h). Then write full sentences.

1 have tea / evening   ○   ○ a big stores / less friendly
2 swimming   ○   ○ b coffee / keep me awake
3 have one long vacation ○   ○ c commuting / expensive
4 a job nearer to home   ○   ○ d go / the gym / too tiring
5 rent than buy   ○   ○ e not sure / stay here
6 reading the news online ○   ○ f it / more up-to-date
7 small stores   ○   ○ g travel / farther
8 driving a small car   ○   ○ h use / less gas

1 *b; I prefer to have tea in the evening because coffee keeps me awake.*
2 _____
3 _____
4 _____
5 _____
6 _____
7 _____
8 _____

3 Pronunciation rising and falling intonation

▶ **49** Listen and repeat the questions. Notice how the intonation rises then falls.

1  2

3  4

4 Listen and respond preferences

▶ **50** Listen to the questions. Respond with your own answer, giving a reason for your preference. Then compare your response with the model answer that follows.

Do you usually take the bus or walk?

I prefer to walk because it's better for me.

7e A great place

Writing a description of a place

1 Read the introduction to a webpage. Then read the information about Amsterdam that a website reader has prepared. Match the website ideas (1–7) with the information (a–g).

a cycling around town or into the nearby countryside. Rowing on the Amstel River is also a popular sport among the locals. ____

b how cosmopolitan it is. **As** almost 200 different nationalities live here, it's a very vibrant town with a wide range of cultural activities every day of the year … and all that within a village-like setting! ____

c it's one of the most multi-faceted cities in the world. Its cosmopolitan landscape, liberal mentality, world-class museums, stunning canals, and fascinating history merge to exude a unique charm that's simply captivating. ____

d on the bridge that crosses the Groenburgwal Canal. Amsterdam is very photogenic, and there are many great spots for a memorable picture. ____

e the Begijnhof in the heart of Amsterdam—a tranquil place with beautiful houses and trees. It's simply the most magical place. ____

f the tallest men. The Dutch are some of the tallest people on this planet. ____

g the Van Gogh Museum (I'm a big fan of Van Gogh). But there are many others, **like** the Rijksmuseum with its stunning collection of Rembrandts. ____

Welcome to another edition of **I Love My City**. This week we have an insider's tour of **Amsterdam**.

Want to see your city on **Intelligent Travel**? Copy and paste our list of fill-in-the-blank ideas into an email, fill in your answers, and send your responses (with any photos, videos, or links) to IntelligentTravel@ngs.org.

1 The first place I take a visitor from out of town is …
2 If you come to my city, get your picture taken …
3 In my city, an active day outdoors involves …
4 My city's best museum is …
5 The most unexpected thing about my city is …
6 My city has …
7 My city should be featured on your website because …

2 Writing skill organizing ideas

Match these categories (1–3) with the information (a–g) in Exercise 1.

1 places to see _____, _____
2 things to do _____, _____
3 general information _____, _____, _____

3 Word focus *as* and *like*

a Look at the highlighted words in the article. Circle the correct option.

1 as = *because / such as*
2 like = *because / such as*

b Complete the sentences about Amsterdam with *as* or *like*.

1 _____ there are so many museums, there's lots to do on a rainy day.
2 Places _____ Amsterdam are full of surprises.
3 _____ it's so photogenic, it attracts lots of photographers.
4 People here love outdoor activities _____ cycling and rowing.
5 It's great for cycling _____ it's so flat.

4 Use the ideas in the article to write about your own town or city.

Wordbuilding noun → adjective

> ▶ **WORDBUILDING noun → adjective**
>
> We can make adjectives from nouns by adding a suffix such as -al or -ic. Spelling changes are sometimes needed.
>
> *nature → natural, person → personal, artist → artistic*

1 Add -al or -ic to these nouns to make adjectives. Make spelling changes where necessary.

1 artist: _____
2 benefit: _____
3 center: _____
4 coast: _____
5 economy: _____
6 energy: _____
7 fact: _____
8 finance: _____
9 history: _____
10 music: _____
11 nation: _____
12 origin: _____
13 profession: _____
14 romance: _____
15 tradition: _____
16 type: _____

2 Complete the sentences with adjectives from Exercise 1.

1 Do you know how to play any _____ instruments, like the guitar or the piano?
2 I used to read a lot of _____ novels, but now I prefer mysteries.
3 I'm not very good with money or _____ problems.
4 My neighbor used to be a _____ soccer player. He played for Argentina.
5 My sister has always been _____ . She won prizes at school for her drawings.
6 Rain and snow are _____ Canadian weather in the winter.
7 What colors are the _____ flag of Japan?

Learning skills understanding new words in context

When you come across a new word, you can often guess its meaning. If you have a dictionary handy, you can look it up. However, many English words have several meanings. It helps if you can work out the relationship of the word to the other words in the sentence.

3 Look at the words in bold in these sentences that are connected with Student Book page 87. Is each word an adjective (A), a noun (N), or a verb (V)?

1 The government transformed the **mining** zone into a national park. ____
2 As a child, I used to spend all my time **carrying** water. ____
3 Dofia Lala was **working** as a maid when she met the love of her life. ____
4 The shop filled with **working**-class men. ____
5 ... **nodding** to the music. ____
6 I played the **recording** for my father. ____

4 Read these paragraphs. Are the words in bold adjectives (A), nouns (N), or verbs (V)?

This is my village. The main [1] **building** in the village _____ is the community center. My house stands next to a [2] **rushing** river. We have a big family [3] **gathering** here _____ this weekend. _____

It's Sunday evening in the city. There's a free concert in the park. Workmen are [4] **building** the stage and _____ everyone's [5] **rushing** around. The technicians are _____ checking the lights in the [6] **gathering** darkness. _____

Check!

5 Answer these questions. The first letter of each answer spells a word. What is it?

1 This is the biggest city in the U.S.
2 If you want to buy or sell a house, go to a real _____ agent.
3 Made up of different nationalities.
4 You might stay in one of these in Mongolia.
5 The natural environment of animals or plants.
6 Something modern houses are often made from. They are usually red or brown.
7 On a sunny day, it's nice to leave the house and go here.
8 An option if you don't want to buy a house.
9 Extremely tall buildings.

1	
2	
3	
4	
5	
6	
7	
8	
9	

Unit 8 Travel

8a Business or pleasure?

Vocabulary vacation activities

1 Complete the vacation activities with these words.

going	hiking	lying	playing	riding	visiting

1 _____ a bike, a camel, a pony
2 _____ volleyball, board games, cards
3 _____ cities, famous monuments, theme parks
4 _____ climbing, sailing, sightseeing
5 _____ in the forest, in the mountains, on a trail
6 _____ around the pool, on a sunbed, on the beach

2 Vocabulary extra *travel* or *trip*

Complete the sentences with the correct form of *travel* or *trip*.

1 I've just gotten back from an amazing _____ to Greece.
2 We _____ right across Australia. It took a week.
3 I love going on long train _____ .
4 We went on a few day _____ from the resort.
5 Do you have any _____ plans for the summer?
6 Air _____ is fast, but it's usually pretty expensive.

Listening a travel journalist

3 ▶ 51 Listen to an excerpt from a radio program about travel journalist Boyd Matson. Circle the correct answers. More than one may be correct. (a–c).

1 Boyd Matson travels mainly
   a in his work.
   b for pleasure.
   c for family reasons.

2 He became interested in traveling
   a a long time ago.
   b recently.
   c when he worked for NBC News.

3 He thinks that travel can be
   a dangerous.
   b fun.
   c expensive.

4 His attitude to travel is that it's best to
   a avoid danger.
   b observe people.
   c take part in things.

4 ▶ 51 Listen again. Complete the sentences.

1 Matson usually manages to find _____ on his trips.
2 He never seems to take these _____ too seriously.
3 Working for NBC News, he spent _____ his time traveling and reporting from places that were in the news.
4 You have to be careful not to take unnecessary risks in _____ like Everest.
5 Now that Matson has a _____ , he doesn't travel quite as often as before.
6 He describes his travel philosophy as "get off the tour _____ ."

dehydration (n) /ˌdiːhaɪˈdreɪʃn/ when you do not have enough water in your body

Grammar verb patterns: *-ing* form and infinitive

5 Complete the sentences with the *-ing* form or infinitive form of the verbs.

1 _____ (fly) isn't as expensive as it used to be.

2 It's easy _____ (buy) airline tickets online these days.

3 Guided tours are a fun way of _____ (find out) about famous places.

4 It's sometimes difficult _____ (decide) where to stay.

5 If you enjoy _____ (speak) languages, foreign vacations are a great chance to practice.

6 For a lot of people, _____ (relax) is the main aim of a vacation.

7 Flying can be stressful when air traffic controllers threaten _____ (go) on strike.

8 _____ (stay) at home can be just as much fun as a foreign vacation.

6 Complete the conversation with the *-ing* form or infinitive form of the verbs.

A: Have you done a lot of [1] _____ (travel)?

B: Well, that depends what you mean by "a lot." I've been to about six or seven countries, I suppose. I enjoy [2] _____ (go) back to my favorite places as often as I can.

A: Seven is a lot! What was your best trip?

B: Probably Iceland, last year. I managed [3] _____ (take) some fantastic photos.

A: Oh, I've always wanted [4] _____ (go) there. I'd love [5] _____ (see) those hot springs that bubble out of the ground.

B: The geysers? Yeah, I really loved [6] _____ (get) close to them. We saw one that shot up about twenty meters! [7] _____ (wait) for them to go really high is great fun.

A: Was that the most spectacular thing you've seen?

B: No, that would probably be Las Vegas. I was very excited about [8] _____ (fly) over the city at night.

7 Circle the correct option.

1 I *expected / mentioned* seeing my uncle.

2 We *enjoyed / wanted* to go to the museum.

3 The guide was really *good at / happy to* explain things.

4 Can you *afford / imagine* living here all year?

5 I rarely *plan / get tired of* visiting new cities.

6 We *refused / worried about* standing for the whole train trip.

8 Rewrite the sentences from Exercise 7 with the other verbs.

1 I _____ my uncle.

2 We _____ the museum.

3 The guide was really _____ things.

4 Can you _____ here all year?

5 I rarely _____ new cities.

6 We _____ for the whole train trip.

9 **Grammar extra** *remember*, *stop*, and *try*

> ▶ **REMEMBER, STOP, and TRY**
>
> Both the *-ing* form and infinitive can follow these verbs, but there is a change in meaning.
>
> *Stop* + *-ing* refers to the **activity** which stops:
>   *I only **stop worrying** when I get off the plane.*
>
> *Stop* + infinitive refers to the reason for stopping:
>   *I never **stop to look** at the view when I'm driving.*

Complete the sentences with the *-ing* form or infinitive form of the verbs.

1 When I'm on vacation, I stop _____ (worry) about things.

2 When we see a nice bar, we stop _____ (have) a drink and a snack.

3 I usually remember _____ (pack) everything I need.

4 I remember _____ (visit) Rome with my father years ago.

5 I'm trying _____ (find) a way to learn Chinese in a month.

6 I've tried _____ (do) an online course, and it helped me a lot.

8b Where to go, what to do there

Reading top movie locations

1 Read the article about taking vacations in movie locations. Circle the activities the article mentions. Where can you do these things?

1 stay in a famous hotel
2 go on a tour with a local guide
3 go up in a hot-air balloon
4 visit a movie studio
5 go sightseeing in the Old Town
6 take a walking tour

2 Read the article again. Answer the questions.

1 What kind of movies were made in Monument Valley?

_____

2 Who lives in Monument Valley?

_____

3 Why is it a good idea to see Monument Valley from the air?

_____

4 How long has Hollywood been making movies in Prague?

_____

5 Why is it easier to get to Prague than it was before?

_____

6 Where can you find more information about London movie locations?

_____

Seen the movie? See the real place!

This is the first in our week-long focus on the best vacation spots for movie fanatics. As a vacation idea, it's more popular than ever, and it's getting easier and easier to find out where your favorite movies were filmed.

Our first destination is Monument Valley, the home of a thousand westerns. When you drive into Monument Valley, you really do feel as if you are stepping onto the set of a cowboy movie. Movie directors have been making westerns here since the 1930s, and the huge red sandstone rock formations have provided the scenery for movies as different as *Stagecoach* in 1939 and *Thelma and Louise* in 1991. Monument Valley covers an area of Arizona and Utah, and although it looks very remote, it's actually easy to get to. Navajo families have lived there for generations, and a lot of Monument Valley is protected land. If you want to take a tour, the best way is to go with a Navajo guide. A trip to Monument Valley is all about the scenery, and so one fun idea is to take a hot-air balloon trip over the valley. A local business there has been running these tours every summer for a few years now. That's the way to go!

And for somewhere completely different from the emptiness of Arizona, try Prague. It's a very atmospheric city, and ever since Hollywood "discovered" Prague in the 1990s, this beautiful and vibrant place has been attracting a lot of action heroes. Tom Cruise was here to film *Mission Impossible*, and Wesley Snipes chased vampires through the Old Town in *Blade II*. Prague has always been one of Europe's main cultural centers, so there's a lot to see, including museums, castles, and fantastic architecture. In the last few years airlines have been adding more flights and more connections, so it's really easy to get there.

Tomorrow we'll focus on London with information about walking tours through the settings of *Notting Hill*, *Shakespeare in Love*, and *Bridget Jones*. We also feature a family treat for Harry Potter fans at King's Cross Station.

sandstone (n) /ˈsænstəʊn/ rock which is made of sand
Navajo (n) /ˈnɑvəhəʊ/ a Native American tribe

Grammar present perfect, present perfect continuous, and *How long … ?*

3 Complete the comments from visitors to the film locations. Use the present perfect and the present perfect continuous forms of the verbs.

1 We _____ (walk) around London all day—we _____ (see) every Harry Potter site!

2 The guide _____ (tell) us about the film stars he _____ (meet).

3 I _____ (take) photos of this amazing scenery, but my battery _____ (just / run out).

4 We _____ (wait) for the weather to change so the balloon can take off—we _____ (pay) for our tickets already.

5 I _____ (explore) Buenos Aires on my own. I _____ (find) some quiet, pretty corners.

6 Let's get a coffee. We _____ (not / have) anything to drink and we _____ (sightsee) since 8 a.m.

4 Rewrite the sentences using the words in parentheses. Use the present perfect or present perfect continuous, as appropriate.

1 I came to the beach after breakfast. Now it's dinnertime.
   I've been lying on the beach all day.
   (lie / all day)

2 We set off at seven. It's now three o'clock.
   _____
   (travel)

3 We first came here ten years ago. We come every year.
   _____
   (come)

4 I started this book when I arrived. I haven't finished it yet.
   _____
   (read)

5 I left Denver this morning. Now I'm in L.A.
   _____
   (drive / over 1,000 miles)

6 This is our third hotel on this vacation!
   _____
   (stay)

5 Write questions with *How long* and the present perfect continuous for sentences 1–4 in Exercise 4. Then write the answers.

1 _____
   _____

2 _____
   _____

3 _____
   _____

4 _____
   _____

6 Dictation *How long … ?*

▶ **52** Listen and write the questions. Then complete the answers for yourself.

1 Q: _____
   A: _____

2 Q: _____
   A: _____

3 Q: _____
   A: _____

4 Q: _____
   A: _____

5 Q: _____
   A: _____

PLATFORM 9¾

8c Travel questions

Listening a radio show

1 ▶ 53 You are going to listen to a radio show about typical travel advice. Circle the words you think you will hear. Then listen and check.

seat	delays	standards	refreshments
ticket	visas	flexibility	low-cost airlines
resorts	insurance	toothache	package vacations

2 ▶ 53 Listen again. Complete the questions that the expert gives advice on.

1 Are low-cost airlines as reliable as big _____ ?

2 Can you save money if you buy _____ directly from the airline?

3 Do I really need to buy travel _____ ?

3 What answers did the expert give? Circle the correct option (a or b).

1 a It's better to fly with the bigger airlines.
   b You have the same rights with big and small airlines.
2 a Booking directly doesn't necessarily save money.
   b You'll always find cheaper prices through travel agents.
3 a Insurance is a good idea for some places.
   b You should always buy travel insurance.

Word focus *thing*

4 Match the excerpts from the radio program (1–4) with the uses of the expressions with *thing* (a–d).

1 People are arranging the kinds of things that travel agents always used to do. ____
2 The thing is, the travel insurance seems really expensive. ____
3 The things that can go wrong don't need to be dramatic. ____
4 The most important thing to do before going on vacation is to get good travel insurance. ____

a giving advice
b introducing a problem or explanation
c talking about general examples of something
d referring to a group of unspecified ideas, objects, etc.

5 Complete the sentences with these expressions with *thing*.

a few things	and things	best thing
important thing	sort of thing	worst thing

1 I love visiting old churches _____ .
2 We're almost ready to go. I just need to sort _____ out.
3 The _____ about this kind of garbage is that it takes years to disappear.
4 She's really into conservation and that _____ .
5 The _____ about France is the food.
6 The _____ is to check with the tour operator.

6 Vocabulary extra synonyms

Look at these words from the radio program. Match pairs of words with a similar meaning.

~~airlines~~	article	package deals
budget	~~companies~~	low-cost
queries	questions	report
package vacations		

_____*airlines = companies*_____

_____

_____

_____

_____

8d Is something wrong?

Vocabulary travel problems

1 Make compound nouns with these words.

allowance	control	documents	pass
poisoning	rental	room	schedule

1 baggage _____
2 boarding _____
3 car _____
4 food _____
5 hotel _____
6 passport _____
7 travel _____
8 train _____

2 Complete the sentences with the compound nouns from Exercise 1.

1 I left the _____ at home, so I hope the times are on our tickets.
2 You can't go back now—you've been through _____ .
3 Our _____ is right above the hotel kitchen!
4 Did they write the gate number on the _____ when we checked in?
5 We had to pay extra because we went over our _____ .
6 I have some medicine with me in case I get _____ .
7 Excuse me, where are the _____ offices? Are they outside?
8 Keep all your _____ in a safe place.

Real life dealing with problems

3 Match the comments (1–6) with the responses (a–f). Circle the things a tourist would say.

1 Can I help you? ____
2 Why have we been waiting so long? ____
3 I wonder if you could help us? ____
4 Can you do something about the air-conditioning? ____
5 I'm sorry, but I lost the key to my room. ____
6 Is something wrong? ____

a Don't worry. I'll give you another one.
b I hope so. It's about the noise next door.
c Sure. I'll ask someone to take a look at it.
d Yes, I left my bag with all my travel documents somewhere.
e Yes, of course. What's the problem?
f I'm afraid the flight has been delayed.

4 Pronunciation strong and weak forms

▶ 54 Complete the exchanges with these prepositions. Then listen and repeat.

at	for	from

1 A: Which gate are you _____ ?
　 B: I'm _____ Gate 17.
2 A: Where did these people come _____ ?
　 B: They're _____ the other bus—it broke down.
3 A: How long are you here _____ ?
　 B: _____ another week.

5 Listen and respond travel situations

▶ 55 Listen to comments in travel situations. Respond with your own words using the word in parentheses. Then compare your response with the model answer that follows.

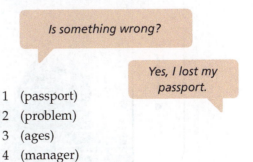

Is something wrong?

Yes, I lost my passport.

1 (passport)
2 (problem)
3 (ages)
4 (manager)
5 (hope)

8e Hello from Egypt!

Writing a text message

1 Writing skill informal style

a What do these informal expressions mean? Write them in the correct place.

Awesome!	Cool!	No way!	Wow!

1 I don't believe it / you. _____
2 I'm surprised. _____
3 I agree / approve. _____
4 That's incredible / amazing / impressive. _____

b What do these abbreviations mean? Write them in the correct place.

BF	GF	LOL	xoxo	thx

1 thank you: _____
2 hugs and kisses (to end a message): _____
3 laugh out loud (to say you found something funny): _____
4 boyfriend: _____
5 girlfriend: _____

c Add exclamation marks to these sentences where appropriate.

1 The resort is fine.
2 The beach is gorgeous.
3 The trip was exhausting.
4 I'm pretty tired.
5 I love it here.

d Rewrite these sentences from a text message as full sentences.

1 Food here delicious.
_____
2 Been on a camel ride (bumpy!).
_____
3 Never been so hot in my life!
_____
4 Taking it easy today cos did too much yesterday.
_____
5 Photos in the usual place online.
_____

e Rewrite these sentences in a more informal style.

1 The weather here is fantastic.
_____
2 We've been lying by the hotel pool since we arrived.
_____
3 I'm thinking of staying an extra week because it's so beautiful.
_____
4 We've arranged to go on a couple of day trips.
_____
5 We had a terrible flight. There was a long delay, the seats were uncomfortable, and there was no food!
_____

2 Write a text message from Egypt. Use the questions as a guide.

- What was the trip there like?
- What's the weather like?
- What's the hotel like?
- What are the people like?
- What's the food like?

Wordbuilding compound nouns (noun + noun)

> ▶ **WORDBUILDING compound nouns (noun + noun)**
>
> We can use two nouns together to mean one thing.
> *baggage allowance, car rental*
>
> Compound nouns can be made up of two words (*boarding pass*), one word (*backpack*), or two words with a hyphen (*man-child*). The plural is made by making the second noun plural (*hotel rooms,* not *hotels room*).

1 Write the compound nouns in three groups.

Accommodations

At the airport

Vacations

Things to pack

arrivals hall	hand luggage
baggage claim	insect repellent
budget hotel	money belt
campsite	sunscreen
departure lounge	travel pills
guest house	youth hostel

2 Write the names of these things.

1 Essential if you want to avoid itchy bites: _____

2 Good value accommodations and not just for young people: _____

3 Not very luxurious, and you need your own tent: _____

4 Where you pick up your luggage after leaving the plane: _____

5 You can take this on the plane: _____

6 A good idea if you are in dangerous areas: _____

7 Don't forget to put this on exposed areas of skin: _____

Learning skills dictionary skills

3 Complete the dictionary definitions with the word they define: *travel* or *trip*.

1 _____ (n) (countable) the act of going somewhere and coming back again, usually for a short time *We've been on a day _____ to the capital.*
2 _____ (v) to go from one place to another, usually in a vehicle *We _____ by train a lot when we were in India.* (n) (uncountable) the activity of visiting different places *They say _____ is good for you.*

4 Check the meaning of *tour* and *voyage* in your dictionary if necessary. Then complete the sentences.

1 I've been on a sightseeing _____ around the island.

2 The _____ across the Indian Ocean took a couple of weeks.

3 We did a walking _____ of London and saw lots of famous places.

4 I've been reading about James Cook's first _____ to the Pacific.

Check!

5 Solve the anagrams to find words from Student Book Unit 8.

1 `a` `d` `e` `l` `s` `y`
you often get them at airports: _____

2 `e` `e` `g` `g` `h` `i` `i` `n` `s` `s` `t`
visiting famous monuments, etc: _____

3 `a` `b` `d` `o` `r` `a` `e` `g` `m` `s`
you can play these on rainy days: _____

4 `a` `e` `c` `l` `m`
you can ride on one: _____

5 `a` `e` `e` `h` `r` `t` `w`
everyone wants this to be good when they're on vacation: _____

6 `c` `e` `i` `k` `t` `t`
you can't travel without buying one: _____

7 `c` `e` `i` `m` `o` `o` `r` `s` `t` `u`
low-impact travel: _____

8 `a` `d` `e` `i` `i` `n` `n` `o` `s` `t` `t`
the place you go to: _____

9a Gift items

Listening choosing a gift

1 ▶ 56 Listen to the conversation between two sisters who are choosing a gift for their aunt. Circle one or more options (a–c).

1 What are they looking for on the internet?
   a unusual presents
   b luxury gifts
   c special deals

2 What kind of jewelry does their aunt wear?
   a a gold chain
   b earrings
   c gold rings

3 What does the GoodWeave logo mean?
   a the carpets aren't made by children
   b the carpets aren't made in factories
   c the factories have been inspected

4 What kind of silk items do they consider?
   a kimonos
   b tablecloths
   c wall hangings

> **logo** (n) /ˈləʊgəʊ/ a picture or design that represents an organization
> **wall hanging** (n) /wɔːl ˈhæŋɪŋ/ fabric with a design or picture that can go on the wall like a painting
> **hand-woven** (adj) /hænd'wəʊvn/ describes a fabric or material that is made by hand
> **weave** (v) /wiːv/ to make threads into fabric

2 ▶ 56 Listen again. Match the gift ideas (a–c) with the sentences.

a pieces of jewelry
b carpets
c antique silk wall hangings

1 These are no longer produced. ____
2 These are being made following traditional methods. ____
3 These can be made to your individual design. ____
4 These have been chosen for their quality. ____
5 These are imported from the people who make them. ____

Grammar passives

3 Read about each product. Circle the correct option.

At this workshop in Kolkata, delicate gold necklaces for weddings [1] *are assembling / are being assembled*. Each piece [2] *contains / is contained* up to 45 grams of gold. According to the merchant, they [3] *will buy / will be bought* mostly for brides from low-income families.

In Azerbaijan, carpets [4] *have made / have been made* by hand for centuries. Both wool and silk [5] *use / are used*, and popular designs [6] *include / are included* birds, animals, and scenes from daily life.

4 Vocabulary extra adjectives

Look at these descriptions. Underline the adjectives that give factual information. Circle the adjectives that give opinions. Which type of adjective comes first?

1 a nice plain gold chain
2 beautiful traditional hand-woven rugs
3 gorgeous antique silk wall hangings

5 Add these factual adjectives to the table.

19th-century	blue	hand-made	Italy	large
mass-produced	old	plastic	tiny	wool

1	How big?	
2	How old?	antique
3	How is it made?	hand-woven
4	What color?	
5	Where from?	China
6	Material?	gold, silk

Silk is a highly versatile and decorative textile. Because of its price, it [7] *has often associated / has often been associated* with luxury goods. Nowadays, more and more synthetic materials [8] *are substituting / are being substituted* for silk.

6
Rewrite these sentences with the adjectives. Use the same order (1–6) as in the table in Exercise 5.

1 The factory makes toys. (plastic / mass-produced)
_____
_____

2 It's a wall hanging. (silk / 19th century)
_____
_____

3 We bought a rug at the sale. (blue / wool)
_____
_____

4 She usually wears earrings. (gold / large)
_____

5 It's a box. (Italian / tiny)
_____
_____

6 We've got some chairs in the garden. (metal / old)
_____
_____

7 Dictation describing objects

▶ 57 Listen and write the information about an object. When you hear "period" this means you have reached the end of a sentence. Then look at the photos and decide which object is being described.

1 _____
2 _____
3 _____
4 _____
5 _____

Vocabulary shopping (1)

1 Complete the sentences with these words.

afford	budget	checkout
deals	goods	purchases
special offer	value for money	

1 I bought my tablet because there was a
_____ of ten percent off.

2 In some places, the stores wrap your
_____ if they're gifts.

3 I can't _____ to go out much this
month—I need to save for my vacation.

4 Some students don't know how to create a
_____ , so they run out of money.

5 I've had this jacket for five years. It's been
great _____ .

6 Most stores give you a full refund on faulty
_____ .

7 I always realize I've forgotten something
when I get to the _____ at the
supermarket.

8 My sister got some great _____ on
her insurance and phone contracts when she
renewed them.

Grammar articles and quantifiers

2 Read the article about passwords and circle the
correct options.

3 Read the article again. Answer the questions.

1 What two characteristics should a password
have?

_____

2 Who is Mark Burnett?

_____

3 What should a password contain in addition to
lowercase letters?

_____

4 What is the list of codes with the article?

_____

Passwords

These days, almost everyone uses [1] *a / the* computerized system for at least [2] *many / one or two* things: perhaps [3] *the online banking / online banking* and [4] *the cash machines / cash machines*. So they probably have to try and remember [5] *a little / several*

1	123456
2	password
3	12345678
4	1234
5	-----*
6	12345
7	dragon
8	qwerty
9	696969
10	mustang

passwords. In theory, you should use a unique and secret password for each different thing. But security expert Mark Burnett says that [6] *too many / too much* people are terrible at choosing personalized passwords and only [7] *a few / several* people keep their passwords secret. It only takes [8] *a few / a little* time and effort to come up with an efficient password, but there are [9] *any / plenty of* us who simply don't do it.

Look closely at [10] *a / the* list of passwords shown here. Are [11] *any / a little* of them familiar to you? They seem obvious and predictable, don't they? Well, these are the ten most commonly used passwords in [12] *the world / world*. If you want your online transactions to be secure, then give it [13] *a little / a couple of* thought and make a password that has [14] *few / one or two* numbers and [15] *any / some* uppercase letters, as well as lowercase letters. Don't choose [16] *the dates / dates* or numbers that are easy to guess and never tell anyone what your passwords are.

* Not appropriate to publish in this book—too rude.

4 Correct the mistakes in these sentences. There is either an incorrect or missing article or quantifier in each sentence.

1 I saved much money by not eating in a café every day.

2 When you're studying, the time management is really important.

3 My friend has been working as waitress in a coffee shop this month.

4 We couldn't get into the exhibition because there were plenty of people there.

5 OK, I'll be ready to go in few minutes.

6 A friend gave me a really good advice about making a budget.

7 I always look online first when I'm thinking about buying the electrical goods.

8 I need a little more days to finish the work.

5 Grammar extra reflexive and reciprocal pronouns

> **REFLEXIVE and RECIPROCAL PRONOUNS**
>
> We use reflexive pronouns when the subject and object are the same:
> *I bought myself a CD.* (not *I bought me*) = the CD is for me
> *I bought him a CD.* = the CD is for someone else
>
> We use reflexive pronouns when we want to emphasize that the subject did something alone:
> *I did it myself.*
>
> We use the reciprocal pronoun *each other* when more than one person does the same thing:
> *They all looked at each other, waiting for someone to speak.*

a Circle the correct option.

1 We bumped into *each other / ourselves* in the supermarket.

2 Did you carry all those bags *each other / yourselves*? They look really heavy.

3 They sent *each other / themselves* a card on their birthdays.

4 When did you two first meet *each other / yourselves*?

5 Did Alessandro arrange the concert *himself / itself*?

6 I went to Martina's party, so I bought *her / herself* a present.

7 They saved up and paid for everything *each other / themselves*.

b ▶ 58 Complete the sentences with a reflexive pronoun or *each other*. Then listen and check.

1 My dad made _____ an egg sandwich.

2 I saw _____ reflected in the store window.

3 Sue and I phone _____ every day.

4 She bought _____ another beautiful outfit!

5 It's his own business, so he pays _____ very well.

6 They looked at _____ across the table.

6 Pronunciation linking

a Write the word that comes before these words in Exercise 5b.

1 _____ egg
2 _____ in
3 _____ I
4 _____ outfit
5 _____ own
6 _____ at

b ▶ 58 Listen again and repeat the sentences.

9c Trade routes

Listening trade routes

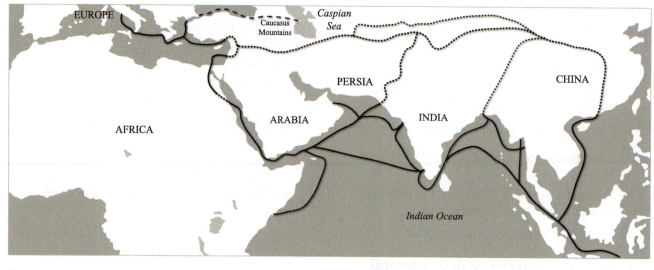

EUROPE
Caucasus Mountains
Caspian Sea
PERSIA
CHINA
ARABIA
INDIA
AFRICA
Indian Ocean

1 You are going to listen to a radio show about trade routes. Before you listen, find the following places on the map.

Arabia	Caucasus Mountains	Europe
Caspian Sea	China	India

2 ▶ 59 Listen to the radio show. Match the routes on the map (1–3) with their names (a–c).

1 ———— ○ ○ a The BTK railway

2 – – – – ○ ○ b The Silk Road

3 ·········· ○ ○ c The Spice Route

black pepper

cinnamon

cardamom

ginger

> **driving force** (n) /ˈdraɪvɪŋ fɔːs/ the reason for or power behind a change
> **echo** (n) /ˈekəʊ/ a repetition of something, usually a sound

3 ▶ 59 Listen again. Write letters (a–c) for the route and draw arrows for the direction.

		Route a BTK b Silk Road c Spice Route	Direction East to West ◄— West to East —►
1	oil products	___	◄—
2	European goods	b	___
3	precious stones	___	___
4	glassware	b	___
5	perfumes	b	___
6	paper	___	___
7	ceramics	___	___
8	black pepper	___	___

Word focus *much*

4 Look at two uses of *much* from the radio show. Then insert *much* in the correct position in the sentences.

"Much of this epic railway has already been built." = *much* + *of* + noun (quantity)

"The sea trade routes […] became much more important." = *much* + comparative adjective (comparison)

1 How did it cost you?

2 I've spent far too money today.

3 She always uses too perfume, I think.

4 I haven't had time to go shopping recently.

5 Oh, that's too expensive!

6 I can get this cheaper online.

9d It's on sale

Real life buying things

1 Read the first line of these exchanges between a customer (C) and a salesperson (S). Write the responses using the words in parentheses.

1 S: We have several models. Here are some of our most popular ones.

   C: _____ ?

   (can / one / at / look / I)

2 C: How much is this one?

   S: _____ .

   (for / sale / it's / $30 / on)

3 S: Do you like this one?

   C: _____ .

   (no / more / something / I / modern / want)

4 S: Can I help you?

   C: _____ ?

   (yes / dining room / where's / section / the)

5 C: I'm looking for a table I saw on your website.

   S: _____ ?

   (have / reference number / you / the / do)

6 S: We can deliver it within two days.

   C: _____ ?

   (how much / charge / you / do)

7 C: Do I pay the full amount now?

   S: _____ .

   (yes / pay / by credit card / or / you / can / in cash)

Vocabulary shopping (2)

2 Complete the sentences.

1 I can't get the printer today. They don't have any i_____ s_____ .

2 All the c_____ r_____ are busy. We'll have to wait in line.

3 I bought this sweater, but it's the wrong size. Can I e_____ it for a smaller one?

4 They don't charge much for d_____ , but they only come to my area every two weeks.

5 I can't find it on the website without the r_____ n_____ .

6 Keep the r_____—you might need it to r_____ the clock.

3 Pronunciation silent letters

▶ **60** Say these words and cross out the silent letters. Then listen and check.

eighth	foreign	neighbors
sight	receipt	whale

4 Listen and respond shopping

▶ **61** Listen to the salesperson's questions. Respond with your own words. Then compare your response with the model answer that follows.

Can I help you?

No, thanks. I'm just looking.

9e For sale

Writing customer feedback

1 Read the customer feedback from two online shopping sites. Answer the questions.

   1 Does the feedback give information about the product or the seller, or both?

      _____

   2 Is the feedback mainly positive or negative?

      _____

   3 What are the specific problems in each case?

      _____

   4 Do you think the customers would make the same purchases again?

      _____

2 **Writing skill clarity: pronouns**

a Look at the words in bold in the customer feedback. What do these words refer to?

b Rewrite these sentences from the review to make them clearer. Use the words given.

   1 When they came, one of the bowls was in fact broken. *the bowls / them*

   2 I decided to post this to warn people not to buy from them. *review / this seller*

c Replace some of the nouns in these sentences with pronouns to avoid repetition.

   1 The sweater fits me perfectly, and I love the color. I think the sweater is good value for money.

   2 The vacuum cleaner came with some instructions, but they aren't in English so we can't understand the instructions.

   3 I ordered this bag online. But when the bag came, the bag wasn't what I expected.

3 Look at the notes about two online purchases and write reviews. Use your own ideas to add details.

	1	2
product	DVD	leather boots on sale
problem	scratched, didn't play	–
action	emailed seller	–
comment	replacement sent	perfect fit good quality
recommendation	no	yes

I was a little nervous about ordering glass online. When **they** came, one of the bowls was in fact broken. However, I took a photo of the packaging and emailed **it** to the company and **they** sent two new bowls free of charge. The service was fine in the end, but I don't think I'll buy fragile goods online again.

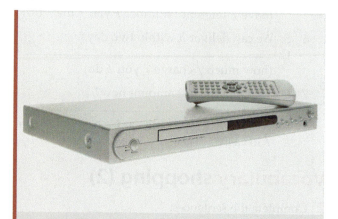

Bought this DVD player because of the low price. Now I know why **it** was so cheap. The cable keeps falling out of the back of the player, and the remote control stopped working after two days. I contacted the seller by email two weeks ago, but **they** still haven't replied. I'll have to call **them**. But I decided to post **this** to warn people not to buy from **them**.

Wordbuilding
compound adjectives

> ▶ **WORDBUILDING compound adjectives**
>
> Compound adjectives are adjectives made of more than one word. The hyphen shows that the words form one adjective.
>
> *duty-free goods, two-day lemon festival*

1 These compound adjectives appear on page 111 of the Student Book. Match them with the nouns they can describe.

1 world-famous:

_____

2 deadly looking:

_____

3 hand-dyed:

_____

4 eight-year-old:

_____

actor	boy	brand	child
knife	leather	silk	weapon

2 Complete the compound adjectives in these sentences with these words.

24	full	hand	life
old	paper	two	vacuum

1 Online banking is a _____-free system.

2 _____-made shoes are very expensive.

3 We went to a _____ -day music festival last week.

4 My new job is a _____-time position.

5 This coffee stores well because it's _____-packed.

6 It's a nice coat, but it's a little _____-fashioned.

7 Save on your phone bill by signing a _____ -month contract.

8 Leaving university was a _____-changing moment for me.

Learning skills recording new words (2)

3 Look at the strategies (a–d). Write notes for these words. Which techniques work best for which words? Does it depend on whether the word is a verb, noun, or adjective?

borrow: _____

_____

merchant: _____

_____

mass-produced: _____

_____

a draw a picture of the word
b write other words connected to this word (opposites, synonyms, words it reminds you of, etc.)
c write where you might read, hear, or use this word
d write a personalized sentence with the word

4 Find six new words in the Student Book or Workbook Unit 9 and write personalized sentences with them.

_____

_____

_____

_____

_____

_____

Check!

5 Write the names of the things.

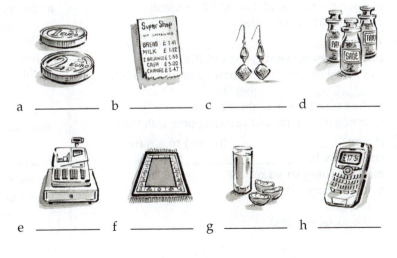

a _____ b _____ c _____ d _____

e _____ f _____ g _____ h _____

Unit 10 No limits

10a A new life

Grammar second conditional

1 Complete the quiz questions with the correct form of the verbs. Then answer the questions for yourself.

How would you cope in a new life?

Take our quick quiz and see how you would do.

1 If you _____ (have to) move to somewhere new, where _____ (you / go)?
   a somewhere more urban than where I live now
   b somewhere with a better climate than where I live now
   c somewhere similar to where I live now

2 Imagine you _____ (take) only one bag with you. What _____ (be) in it?
   a not much—I'd rather get new stuff
   b some practical stuff that might be useful
   c family photos and videos

3 What _____ (you / miss) the most from your old life?
   a it's hard to say without knowing what the new life _____ (be) like
   b the house I live in at the moment
   c seeing my friends and spending time with them

4 If you _____ (move) to a new country, what _____ (be) the hardest thing to adapt to?
   a a new language
   b the food
   c the social customs

5 Do you think you _____ (find) a job easily if you _____ (go) to live somewhere new?
   a yes, I _____ (welcome) the chance to do something new
   b yes, I _____ (probably / do) my type of work anywhere
   c no, I _____ (have to) do something new

6 What _____ (be) the best thing about living in a new place?
   a everything—I _____ (love) to change my life
   b the chance to look at things differently
   c nothing—if I _____ (have) no choice about moving

Answers

Mostly a: You're ready for new horizons! Are you unhappy where you are, or do you just have itchy feet?

Mostly b: You're the kind of person who looks at the pros and cons of a situation. You'd cope well in a new place.

Mostly c: You're a homebody. Are you happy where you are or possibly a little unadventurous? It might not be wise to move somewhere new.

2 Circle the most logical option.

1 If I wanted to study in the U.K., I *would / could / might* have to learn English.

2 If I lost my job, I *would / could / might* be shocked.

3 If you spoke the language, you *would / could / might* ask for help.

4 You never know—you *would / could / might* enjoy it if you tried it.

5 If you could spend a year traveling, where *would / could / might* you go?

6 If I went traveling for a year, there's a chance I *would / could / might* never come home!

3 Complete the conversation with conditionals. Use the words in parentheses.

A: ¹_____ (you / go) on one of those space tourism flights?

B: No! I ²_____ (be) terrified.
I ³_____ (not / go) if you ⁴_____ (pay) me!

A: I think it sounds great. If the tickets ⁵_____ (not / be) so expensive, I ⁶_____ (love) to do that.

B: They ⁷_____ (probably / get) cheaper in the future.

A: OK, if the price ⁸_____ (drop) enough, I ⁹_____ (buy) us two tickets.

Listening **a different climate**

4 ▶ 62 Listen to two colleagues discussing life in different climates. Which five of these ways of dealing with cold and hot climates do they mention?

active lifestyle	daily routines
air conditioning	fires
car technology	food
clothes	swimming pool

5 ▶ 62 Listen again. Complete the sentences with *man* or *woman*.

1 The _____ doesn't like going outside in really cold weather.

2 The _____ tends to eat a lot in a cold climate.

3 The _____ thinks a nap in the middle of the day is a good idea.

4 The _____ doesn't like sleeping during the day.

5 The _____ is pretty happy living where he/she is.

6 Complete these sentences using the second conditional. Who do you think said each one?

1 I _____ (not / enjoy) living in Canada. ___

2 I _____ (feel) cold even if I _____ (wear) high-tech clothes. ___

3 If I _____ (live) in Canada, I _____ (gain) weight. ___

4 I think you _____ (avoid) the heat if you _____ (get up) early. ___

7 Dictation *if …*

▶ 63 Listen and write down the parts of the sentences. Then match the beginnings (1–4) with the endings (a–d) to make complete sentences.

1 _____

2 _____

3 _____

4 _____

a _____

b _____

c _____

d _____

10b Human limits

Reading what can the body take?

1 Read the information on *Human limits*. Write these section headings in the correct places.

Blood Loss	Dehydration	Hot Air
Body Heat	Diving Deep	Lack of Oxygen
Cold Water	High Altitude	Starvation

2 Read the information again. Answer the questions.

1 How long can we survive without food?

_____

2 How long can we survive without water?

_____

3 How long can we survive at 150°C?

_____

4 At what percentage blood loss would we need a transfusion?

_____

5 What's the maximum core body temperature we can withstand?

_____

6 What helps people who live at high altitudes?

_____

Grammar defining relative clauses

3 Complete the sentences by adding a relative pronoun in the correct place. If the relative pronoun is optional, put parentheses ( ) around it. If more than one pronoun is possible, write both.

1 The nurses looked after me were very professional.

_____

2 The operation I had was a simple procedure.

_____

3 The injection the nurse gave me didn't hurt much.

_____

4 The nearest pharmacy opens late is in the town center.

_____

5 The doctor works in our local clinic is great.

_____

6 The ankle I broke last year still hurts.

_____

4 Match the phrases (1–6) and the sentences (a–f). Then rewrite the pairs as one sentence using a relative pronoun beginning with *wh-*. When you've written the sentences, put parentheses ( ) around any optional pronouns.

1 That's the patient _____

_____

2 This is the place _____

_____

3 I can name several famous people _____

_____

4 I talked to the surgeon _____

_____

5 That's the hospital _____

_____

6 It was noon _____

_____

a I came out of the hospital then.
b I read about him.
c They have had cosmetic surgery.
d I fell and broke my arm here.
e She operated on me.
f They do heart transplants there.

5 Pronunciation sentence stress

▶ 64 Listen and repeat the sentences from Exercise 4.

Vocabulary medicine

6 Circle the correct option (a–c) that describes each word.

1 donor
   a a person
   b a place
   c a procedure

2 scan
   a an illness
   b a place
   c a procedure

3 injection
   a a person
   b a cure
   c a procedure

4 radiographer
   a a person
   b a place
   c a treatment

5 stitches
   a an illness
   b a test
   c a procedure

6 ward
   a a person
   b a place
   c a treatment

Health

Human limits

A 64-year-old woman fell on the ice last December. Her arthritis stopped her from getting up. She lay in the snow for hours. Her temperature dropped to 21°C. Her heart stopped. But doctors revived her, and today she is fine. Medical science is always learning more about how much a body can take. Yet as Duke University physician Claude Piantadosi notes, "At some point, it's impossible to rescue yourself." Here's current thinking on the extremes of human endurance.

42°C
1 _____
When core body temperature reaches 42°C, heatstroke can't be reversed and is fatal.

5°C
2 _____
Water saps body heat. You'd last no more than 30 minutes in a 5°C sea. Life vests keep you up to slow heat loss.

150°C
3 _____
In a burning building or a deep mine, adults can withstand 10 minutes at 150°C.

4,500 meters
4 _____
Consciousness fades for most people. With bigger lungs and more red blood cells, highland dwellers are OK.

86 meters
5 _____
Without equipment, most folks black out before 2 minutes and below 18 meters. The best free diver made it to 86 meters.

11 minutes
6 _____
Typically, you'd black out within 2 minutes. With training, people can hold their breath nearly 11 minutes.

40 percent
7 _____
You can survive after losing 30 percent. At 40 percent, you'd need an immediate transfusion.

45 days
8 _____
Lose 30 percent of body weight and death is imminent, though disease will probably kill you before you starve to death.

7 days
9 _____
Every cell needs water. Unless you replace the liter you lose daily, you won't last much more than a week.

10c A limitless brain?

Listening science in movies

1 Look at the photo. What do you think is happening? Circle one of the options (a–c).

a   The weight of the man's brain is being calculated.
b   The man's brain activity is being measured.
c   Scientists are trying to read the man's mind.

2 ▶ 65 Listen to a radio program about movies and science. What's the connection between the movie and the photo?

> **neurologist** (n) /njʊəˈrɒlədʒɪst/ a specialist in the nervous system and the brain

3 ▶ 65 Listen again to what the host says. Answer the questions.

1   What aspect of movies do they look at in this radio program?
_____

2   What does the main character of the movie do?
_____

3   What happens after he does this?
_____

4 ▶ 65 Listen to what the guest says. Use the information you hear to complete the sentences.

1   It's not even _____ that we only use 20 percent of our brain.

2   We use different parts of the brain for different _____ .

3   There are no unused or _____ regions of the brain.

4   It would be incredibly _____ for our bodies to only use 20 percent of the brain.

5   We actually already have _____ brain power.

5 What does the host suggest about the things the movie's character achieved?
_____
_____

Word focus *take*

6 Look at these excerpts (1–3) from the radio program. What do the words in bold mean? Match the excerpts with the expressions (a–d). There is one extra expression.

1   The main character **takes** a special pill. ____
2   … if we knew how to **take advantage of** our brains properly … ____
3   **It doesn't take** a genius to achieve this. ____

a   benefit from or use well
b   consume food or drink
c   carry something
d   it's not necessary

7 Write the meaning of *take* in these sentences.

borrow	carry	invite	lead
react to	steal	travel by	

1   I'm taking my parents to the movies tonight.
_____

2   Someone took my umbrella!
_____

3   Where are you taking me?
_____

4   Is it OK if I take your car tomorrow?
_____

5   If I were you, I'd take some food with you.
_____

6   How did your brother take the bad news?
_____

7   There are no buses. Let's take a taxi.
_____

8 Match the responses to the sentences in Exercise 7.

a   As long as you take care of it. ____
b   He can't take it in, really. ____
c   Here, take mine. I've got a hat. ____
d   It's a surprise. It won't take long. ____
e   It's OK. I can get takeout. ____
f   OK, but make sure it doesn't take the long way around. ____
g   Take enough money for drinks and snacks, too.
____

10d First aid

Vocabulary injuries

1 What has happened in each case? Write sentences.

1 He _____

2 She _____

3 He _____

4 He _____

5 He _____

6 She _____

Real life talking about injuries

2 Match the comments (a–f) with the people (1–6) in Exercise 1. More than one answer is possible.

a I feel kind of sick. ____

b I've been stung. ____

c It hurts when I move it. ____

d It's just a sprain. ____

e It's nothing. ____

f It's really painful. ____

3 This is the conversation the person in picture 6 in Exercise 1 had with a friend after the fall. Put the parts of the conversation in the correct order.

____ a A: Maybe. If I were you, I'd see the nurse.

____ b A: Really? It looks swollen. What about this here?

____ c A: Well, you might have broken it.

____ d A: What happened? Let me see!

____ e B: Do you think so?

____ f B: It doesn't hurt very much.

____ g B: Ow! Yes, OK, that's painful.

4 Give advice to a friend. Choose endings to complete the sentences. Remember to use the correct verb forms.

get / looked at	keep / eye
get / X-ray	put / antihistamine cream
go / see the doctor	put / cream
ignore	wash

1 If I were you, _____

2 You should _____

3 I wouldn't _____

4 You'd better _____

5 Why don't you _____

6 It might be worth _____

7 It's probably best _____

8 Have you tried _____

5 Pronunciation *and*

▶ 66 What do you think is the correct order for each pair of words? Listen and repeat the sentences.

1 This is a _____ way to stop bleeding. (easy / quick)

2 Can you give me your _____ _____ ? (address / name)

3 We can help with all problems, _____ _____ . (big / small)

4 It's all written down in _____ _____ . (black / white)

5 The staff are _____ . (friendly / nice)

6 There's something for everyone, _____ _____ . (old / young)

6 Listen and respond *advice*

▶ 67 Listen to people say what has happened to them. Respond with some advice. Use your own words. Then compare your response with the model answer that follows.

> *I think I was bitten by a mosquito last night.*

> *Why don't you put some of this cream on the bite?*

10e What do you think?

Writing a personal email

1 Writing skill linking ideas

a Read the email. Cross out any options that are incorrect.

Hi Jack,

How are things? Here's something I need your help with. As you know, running is my main hobby. [1] *However, / In fact, / To be honest,* you could say it's my only hobby. [2] *Anyway, / All the same, / Well,* my running partner has decided to enter an ultramarathon next year. [3] *Actually, / Naturally, / Obviously,* he wants me to do it as well. He's very confident that we can both finish it.

[4] *By the way, / Incidentally, / The thing is,* I am not convinced. What would you do? I know you aren't a runner, but [5] *all the same / even so / before I forget* you know me better than anyone.

I suppose I don't want to take the risk! It would be terrible to try and not make it! Anyway, I'd appreciate your thoughts.

Later,

Ali

Send   Cancel

---

b What is Ali asking for advice about? Why does he ask Jack?

_____

_____

c Complete the sentences from Jack's reply with these words. There is more than one possible answer.

anyway	by the way	even so	in fact
incidentally	naturally	obviously	
of course	to be honest	well	

1   I'm sorry it's taken me a while to reply to your email. I've been thinking about what you said, _____ !

2   _____ , I've never been faced with this kind of situation.

3   _____ , doing a race like that is going to be a big challenge.

4   _____ , it's up to you in the end.

2 Rewrite these words from Jack's reply as full sentences.

1   I not know / what / I / do in your position.
   _____

2   Even so, if you / have / right training, you / do it.
   _____

3   As I understand it, you / do race next year if you / decide do it.
   _____

4   That / give you / plenty of time / to prepare and see if / a good idea.
   _____

5   I / sure / you / not regret it.
   _____

6   By the way, we / probably stop by / visit you / next month / if we / go / Seattle.
   _____

3 Use the sentences from Exercises 1c and 2 and your own ideas to complete Jack's reply to Ali's email.

Hi Ali,

_____

_____

_____

You are the only person who knows what your body is capable of. _____

_____

_____

It seems like a great opportunity, so if I was you I would seriously consider it. _____

_____

_____

I'll let you know a couple of days in advance. If you haven't made up your mind, we can talk about the ultramarathon more then.

Regards,

Jack

Wordbuilding suffix *-ful*

> ▶ **WORDBUILDING suffix *-ful***
>
> We can add *-ful* to the end of a noun to mean "full of."
> a *painful* injection

1 Match the adjectives in the list to the descriptions (1–7).

beautiful	careful	cheerful	colorful
harmful	peaceful	powerful	stressful
successful	thoughtful	useful	wonderful

1 someone who thinks about other people a lot
_____

2 someone who pays attention to details
_____

3 someone who is positive and happy
_____

4 something that is very strong or has an effect on you
_____

5 something that can cause injury or damage
_____

6 something that helps you do things
_____

7 something that is attractive to look at
_____

2 Complete the sentences with words from the list in Exercise 1.

1 Modern life can be pretty _____ , but we can learn to take it easy.

2 She always achieves what she aims to do. She's very _____ .

3 It was very _____ of you to remember my birthday! Thanks!

4 What a busy week! We need a _____ and relaxing weekend now.

5 What a _____ day! I had a fantastic time.

6 The houses are really _____—pink, green, blue, and even orange!

Learning skills improving your speaking

If you don't get many opportunities to speak English, you might feel that you can't improve as much as you want to. However, recording yourself and comparing your speaking to models is a very effective way of developing your spoken English. You can record your voice in several ways.

3 Which of these things do you have access to?

a a cell phone   c a video camera

b a computer   d a digital voice recorder

4 Here are some ideas of things you can do.

- Record English speakers from DVDs, the radio, or the internet. Then repeat their words and record yourself.
- Record dialogues and conversations. Then take one of the roles, and repeat and record yourself.
- Try to speak spontaneously for one minute on a topic that interests you (you can use notes to speak from). Record yourself.
- Get together with a friend who is learning English and record dialogues from your textbook.

When you listen to yourself, concentrate on one aspect of your speaking at a time. Then record yourself again and try to improve that aspect.

5 Check (✓) the things you could improve most.

☐ Intonation—is it like an English speaker or like your own mother tongue?

☐ Fluency—do you hesitate a lot? Do you pause in the wrong places?

☐ Do you stress the correct words in a sentence?

☐ Do you stress the correct part of words with several syllables?

☐ Pronunciation of vowel sounds—do they sound like your mother tongue?

☐ Pronunciation of other sounds, such as consonants at the end of words—are you "eating" the wrong sounds?

☐ Vocabulary, grammar, and structure—do you have all the words you need?

Check!

6 Look at the completed word puzzle. Write the clues.

1 _____

2 _____

3 _____

4 _____

5 _____

6 _____

7 _____

1					b	e	e
2					b	i	t	e
3				b	l	a	d	e
4			d	o	c	t	o	r
5		r	e	f	u	g	e	e
6	m	a	r	a	t	h	o	n
7	a	s	t	r	o	n	a	u	t

Unit 11 Connections

11a New media

Vocabulary news

1 Read the headlines. Decide which section of a newspaper the headlines are from. Circle one of the options.

1

> Motor world in shock after tragedy

entertainment / sports section

2

> Ford to cut 4,500 jobs

business section / lifestyle

3

> Pirates kidnap yacht crew in Indian Ocean

politics and society / world news

4

> Hospitals need another 1,000 nurses

national news / world news

5

> Why we welcome changes to the education system

opinion / sports section

6

> Last night's TV: The X Factor

opinion / entertainment

7

> Defense secretary to resign

business section / politics and society

8

> Unions in talks over strike

features / front page

Listening WildlifeDirect

2 ▶ 68 Listen to a radio interview with Jo Makeba. Who are these people? Complete the sentences.

1 Richard Leakey _____
  _____ .
2 Paula Kahumbu _____
  _____ .

3 ▶ 68 Listen again. Circle the correct options (a–c).

1 The host said that _____ .
  a wildlife success stories never made the headlines
  b wildlife issues didn't make headlines
  c wildlife stories were usually disaster stories

2 Jo Makeba said that _____ .
  a we rely too much on traditional media
  b it's easier for people to reach a wide audience these days
  c we don't need traditional media anymore

3 Jo Makeba said that WildlifeDirect was _____ .
  a a way of sending wildlife stories to newspapers
  b a wildlife program about gorillas
  c a website that brought small projects together

4 Jo Makeba told the host that WildlifeDirect _____ .
  a had to stop working on elephant conservation
  b was only based on Facebook these days
  c had changed the way it uses social media

5 Jo Makeba said that _____ .
  a many people had stopped using social media
  b WildlifeDirect used both traditional and social media
  c Paula Kahumbu was a journalist before working in conservation

fund (v) /fʌnd/ to provide money for something
lurid (adj) /ˈljʊərɪd/ sensational and shocking

Paula Kahumbu

Grammar reported speech

4 Rewrite these quotes from the interview using reported speech.

1 "Social media has developed."

Jo Makeba said _____

_____

2 "And what exactly is WildlifeDirect?"

The host asked _____

_____

3 "I remember hearing the story about the gorillas."

The host said _____

_____

4 "People reacted to stories by signing petitions or joining public marches."

Jo Makeba said _____

_____

5 "I think that's a small minority."

Jo Makeba said _____

_____

6 "Paula was also involved in a series of wildlife documentaries."

Jo Makeba said _____

_____

5 Read your friend's words to you. Then complete your comments to them using reported speech.

1 "I don't watch the news."

You said _____

2 "I know how to upload photos."

You told me _____

_____

3 "Have you seen this program before?"

You asked me _____

_____

4 "The documentary has just finished."

You said _____

_____

5 "I'll tell you when the news comes on."

You said _____

_____

6 Dictation **You said ...**

▶ 69 Listen and write the comments. Then match the comments with the pictures (a–f).

1 _____

2 _____

3 _____

4 _____

5 _____

6 _____

11b Mobile technology

Reading innovations in communication

1 Read the article about the innovative system FrontlineSMS. Which paragraphs mention these things?

a two types of communications technology ____

b how FrontlineSMS works ____

c a connection between two systems ____

d an example of the system in action ____

e communications problems facing people in remote areas ____

f one way in which Ken Banks surprised people ____

2 Read the article again. Answer these questions in your own words.

1 According to paragraph 1, what specific problem existed between phones and computers?

_____

2 How exactly did Ken Banks solve this problem?

_____

3 What's different about the way a laptop is used with FrontlineSMS?

_____

4 What kind of people or organizations use the system?

_____

MOBILE TECHNOLOGY and the art of the possible

1 For years, communications technology seemed to operate in two separate worlds. On the one hand, there was phone technology. Cell phones could be used almost anywhere, as long as the phone signal had coverage. And in the early years of the 21st century, there weren't many populated places left outside the reach of a cell phone network. On the other hand, there was the internet. In contrast to phone networks, even today there are many places in the world where you can't find a fast, reliable internet connection—if any connection at all. But while phones could talk to phones, and computers could talk to computers, you couldn't send a simple text message between the two systems.

2 For people in richer countries, who had access to both systems, this may not have been a huge problem. But all over the world there are people in remote areas who have a huge need to share information simply and cheaply. Imagine you are a doctor about to set off on a tour of remote villages. You need a quick and simple way to tell the village health workers, pharmacists, and others that you are on your way, and to find out what specific needs—medicine, equipment—they have. The ideal solution would be to text your messages in bulk, using and storing the information on a low-cost computer. And that wasn't possible before a man named Ken Banks wrote the software that allows phones and computers to communicate with each other. Banks created the system, called FrontlineSMS, after returning from a trip to southern Africa. "I wrote the software in five weeks at a kitchen table," he says. "I made it a generic communications platform that could be used for almost anything, and I made it free."

3 Using FrontlineSMS requires simply any laptop computer and a cell phone (even a fairly old or recycled one), and a cable. "After downloading the free software online, you never need the internet again," Banks explains. "Attach a cell phone to the computer with a cable, type your message on the computer keyboard, select the people you want to send it to from a contact list the software lets you create, and hit *send*. Since it can run off an inexpensive laptop, it works for any organization that wants to use text messaging, even in remote locations with unreliable electricity."

4 One story of how FrontlineSMS works comes from Malawi. A rural healthcare network serving 250,000 people was revolutionized when a college student arrived with a hundred recycled phones and a laptop loaded with the software—saving a thousand hours of doctor time, thousands of dollars in fuel costs, and doubling the number of patients cared for, all in the first few months.

5 Today FrontlineSMS delivers vital information in more than 50 countries. It has been used to monitor elections in several countries and to help communication after earthquakes. But perhaps the most remarkable thing of all is that, having come up with such an innovative solution, Ken Banks didn't sell his idea to a huge multinational communications company. He simply gave it, free, to the people who needed it the most.

3 The article suggests there are several reasons why FrontlineSMS is so popular. Circle the words that apply.

economical	long battery life
exclusive brand	reliable
freely available	simple
fun to use	sophisticated

4 Vocabulary extra communications technology

Complete the sentences with these words and phrases.

cable	network
contact list	online
downloading	send a text message
internet connection	signal
keyboard	write software
launch a website	

1 If your cell phone doesn't have a _____ , you can't make calls.

2 The cell phone _____ covers most places these days.

3 "Texting" means to _____
   _____ .

4 If you want to use broadband, you need a fast and reliable _____ .

5 Computer programmers are people who
   _____ .

6 You need a _____ to connect devices unless you are using Wi-Fi.

7 You can usually update programs by _____ them _____ .

8 You need some kind of _____ if you want to type.

9 Most people store names and numbers in a
   _____ .

10 If you want to reach a big audience, it's a good idea to _____ .

Grammar reporting verbs

5 Write sentences reporting what was said.

1 "I'll find a solution."
   (Ken Banks / promise)
   _____
   _____

2 "Would you like to tell us about your ideas?"
   (the company / invite / Ken Banks)
   _____
   _____

3 "We'll give all our customers ten free texts."
   (the phone company / offer)
   _____
   _____

4 "Please donate text messages."
   (the website / ask / the public)
   _____
   _____

5 "Don't be late for appointments."
   (the doctor / tell / the patients)
   _____
   _____

6 "All hospitals should make arrangements for our visits next week."
   (the officials / remind)
   _____
   _____

6 Complete the responses with the correct form of the verbs.

1 A: It's great that you can send texts with a computer now.
   B: I _____ (not / realize) you _____ (can / not).

2 A: I read his Twitter comments on my laptop.
   B: I _____ (not / know) Twitter _____ (work) on a laptop, just a phone.

3 A: You can't text if you don't have a signal.
   B: Really? I _____ (think) you _____ (can).

4 A: I've sent everyone a message about the party.
   B: I _____ (wonder) if you _____ (send) a text or an email.

7 Pronunciation contrastive stress

▶ 70 Listen and repeat the exchanges from Exercise 6.

11c Words and time

Listening old and new words

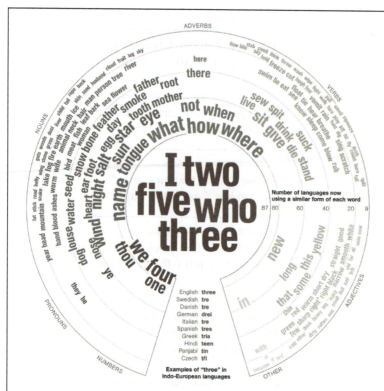

The English versions of two hundred words that have been used since the time of Mesopotamia. The words in the center are the oldest and tend to be similar in different languages. The words near the edge are words that vary between languages and have changed more.

1 You are going to listen to a radio show about how words change over time. Before you listen, look at the diagram and answer the questions.

1 How do you say *three* in Hindi?
_____

2 Which word has been in use longer: *three* or *here*?
_____

3 How many languages today use a similar word for *who*?
_____

2 ▶ 71 Listen to the radio show. On the diagram, circle the words that are mentioned.

> **stable** (adj) /ˈsteɪbl/ unchanging

3 ▶ 71 Listen again. Are the sentences true (T) or false (F)?

1 Mark Pagel looked at words that share a 9,000-year history. T F

2 Pagel analyzed a group of 87 words. T F

3 The words that we use most frequently change the most. T F

4 Verbs and adjectives have changed more quickly than nouns over time. T F

4 What were two advantages of using a computer to analyze the data?
_____
_____

Word focus *time*

5 Look at these excerpts (1–3) from the radio show. In which excerpt do we use *time*:

a with an adjective?

b with a verb?

c as an uncountable noun?

1 How does language change over **time**? ____

2 … have not changed very much since **ancient times** … ____

3 The computer analysis, as well as **taking a lot less time** to look at the data … ____

6 Complete the sentences with these expressions with *time*. There is one extra expression.

all the time	the time
great time	time
have time	time
modern times	years' time
spend time	

1 _____'s up! Please stop writing now and hand in your answer sheets.

2 Do you remember _____ before TV on demand?

3 If you _____ , could you call your sister this evening?

4 Come on, it's _____ to get up.

5 In ten _____ , all books will be digital.

6 My phone's buzzing again! It does it _____ !

7 I think we should _____ with our parents this weekend.

8 Are these ideas relevant in _____ ?

11d Can I take a message?

Real life telephone messages

1 Put the words in order. Then write "A" next to the four sentences from an answering machine message.

a message / this / Nils Davis / is / a / for

_____ .

b Dan's / meeting / I'm / in /afraid / a

_____ .

c delivery / it's / the / of / phone chargers / about

_____ .

d 555-6129 / my / Jill / my number / name's / is / and

_____ .

e take / I / message / can / a

_____ ?

f calling / who's / yes,

_____ ?

g later / you / I'll / try /call / and

_____ .

h let / I'll / called / know / you / him / that

_____ .

2 The other four sentences in Exercise 1 are a receptionist's words in a phone conversation. Complete the conversation with four of the sentences (a–h) from Exercise 1.

C: Hello, can I speak to Dan, please?

R: [1]_____

C: Oh, I'm returning his call.

R: [2]_____

C: Yes, can you ask him to call me?

R: [3]_____

C: It's Alice Black. My number's 555-8824.

R: [4]_____

3 Pronunciation polite requests with *can* and *could*

a ▶ 72 Can you think of more than one way to complete these requests? Listen and write what you hear.

1 Can _____ call _____ back?

2 Could _____ call _____ later?

3 I wonder whether _____ could leave _____ name?

4 Can _____ give _____ _____ number?

5 I wonder if you can tell _____ I called?

6 Could you ask _____ to call me?

b ▶ 72 Listen again and repeat the requests. Pay attention to your intonation.

4 Listen and respond making an appointment

▶ 73 Listen to one half of a conversation between a patient and a doctor's receptionist. You are the receptionist. Respond with your own words using the word in parentheses. Then compare your response with the model answer that follows.

1

> *Can I speak to the doctor, please?*

> *I'm afraid the doctor is with a patient at the moment.*

1 (with a patient)
2 (your name)
3 (new appointment time)
4 (come on Friday)
5 (thank you for calling)

11e A point of view

Writing an opinion essay

1 Read the opinion essay and circle the best title (a–c).

- a Is it easier to learn English these days?
- b Is it essential to learn English in today's world?
- c Why is learning English becoming less popular?

> **1**
> These days, more people than ever are learning English. There are several main reasons why people decide to improve their English skills.
>
> **2**
> First, many people need English in their jobs. Some of them need to speak and write English, but most of them only need to read it. Often, companies say English is a requirement for new employees.
>
> **3**
> Second, the main language of the internet is English. If you want to have access to information, understanding English is a big help. In addition, English is always one of the official languages of international organizations and industries. For example, English is extremely useful in the United Nations or the tourism industry.
>
> **4**
> To sum up, I believe that learning English is essential if you want to be a "citizen of the world."

2 Writing skill essay structure

a Mark the places in the essay where these additional sentences would best fit.

- a I don't think it's a good idea to use automatic translators for this.
- b It depends on the person.
- c So work is one reason why English is necessary.

b Match the paragraphs (1–4) in the essay with these functions (a–d).

- a a short summary of the opinion ____
- b additional ideas or examples ____
- c a general statement which responds to the title ____
- d statements explaining the opinion ____

3 Match these words with the underlined words in the essay.

1 As well as this, _____
2 For instance, _____
3 In conclusion, _____
4 In my opinion, _____
5 Nowadays, _____

4 Complete the table with these words and expressions. Add a comma where necessary.

First	In my opinion
For example	On the other hand
For instance	Nowadays
I believe (that)	Some people say (that)
I disagree (with)	such as
I think (that)	To sum up
In conclusion	

Starting a paragraph	_____ _____ _____ _____
Giving your opinion	_____ _____ _____
Contrasting opinions	_____ _____ _____
Giving examples	_____ _____ _____

5 Read the sentences and decide which essay title in Exercise 1 they match. Then put the sentences in a logical order. ____

- a First, students can watch videos and read newspapers easily online. In addition, they can do courses online. ____
- b In conclusion, all these reasons show that it is easier for English students than it used to be. ____
- c Nowadays, lots of people study English using technology. In my opinion, technology helps students a lot. ____
- d Second, it's easy to speak to other people using technology. ____

6 Add one sentence of your own to each paragraph of the essay in Exercise 5.

Wordbuilding phrasal verbs

> ▶ **WORDBUILDING** phrasal verbs
>
> Phrasal verbs are used frequently in information and communications technology (ICT).
> *I'll **switch off** the computer.*
> *Can you **set up** my email account?*

1 Replace the **bold** words in each sentence with a phrasal verb from this list.

catch up	come up with	find out	turn up
keep up (with)	reach out (to)	set up	
sign out (of)	sum up	switch off	

1 Remember to **disconnect** all devices before you go through airport security. _____

2 Alice has managed to **think of** a fantastic solution to the problem. _____

3 I can't **follow** all of the constant changes at work. _____

4 When did you **hear** about the new schedules? _____

5 I wonder why Matt didn't **appear** for his last exam? _____

6 It's a good idea to **organize** all your favorite programs exactly how you want them. _____

7 You should always **exit from** websites and apps properly when you finish using them. _____

8 It's hard to **summarize** everything that happened in a few words. _____

9 Let's get together soon so we can **get up-to-date** on each other's news. _____

10 We should all talk about this—I'll **contact** Sam and Lia to see when they're free. _____

2 Test your memory. Complete the phrasal verb in each sentence without looking at the list in Exercise 1.

1 I always sign _____ _____ my email on public computers.

2 I hope Sue can come _____ _____ a way of fixing the printer.

3 I just found _____ about the accident.

4 Frances and Nadiya are going to set _____ their own company.

5 Not many people turned _____ for the soccer final.

6 How do you keep _____ _____ all the new developments in IT?

Learning skills using the internet (2)

3 Which of these things have you used the internet for?
- reading the news
- reading about your hobbies or interests
- reading about your job or studies
- researching information for a class

4 Have you done any of the things in Exercise 3 in English? Think of six key terms from your job, studies, or interests. Can you say these words in English? Use the internet to find out.

5 Which of these online resources would you use if you had these problems (1–5)? Match the problems with the online resources.

dictionaries	grammar practice	practice exams
translators	vocabulary practice	

1 How do you say *broadband* in my language?

2 Does the word *unconnected* exist in English?

3 I have to buy some computer gear, but I'm not sure what to ask for in English.

4 I'm still not sure how to report questions.

5 I'm thinking about taking a course to get an official certificate of my level of English.

Check!

6 Can you find eight words in the word square? Use the clues to help you.

1 a kind of message you can send with your cell phone

2 a type of fast internet connection

3 a computer application

4 Facebook and Twitter are examples of social ...

5 the title of a newspaper article

6 up-to-date information

7 when an online video is viewed thousands of times

8 you need this for your cell phone to work

W	T	L	R	G	O	P	E	T	E
H	E	A	D	L	I	N	E	V	Y
C	X	R	P	I	N	E	N	I	S
I	T	S	O	F	T	W	A	R	E
P	W	U	Q	P	Z	S	V	A	A
R	S	K	T	T	I	A	M	L	S
L	C	A	Z	L	L	Q	E	G	L
T	S	I	G	N	A	L	D	D	C
Q	B	G	Z	N	M	U	I	F	T
U	B	R	O	A	D	B	A	N	D

Unit 12 Experts

12a Looking back

Grammar third conditional

1 Match each beginning (1–4) with two endings (a–h). Then write the sentences in the third conditional.

1 If Tim Berners-Lee

_____ (not / invent) the internet,

_____

_____

2 If Alexander Fleming

_____ (not / discover) penicillin,

_____

_____

3 If Dian Fossey

_____

(not / study) mountain gorillas,

_____

_____

4 If Wangari Maathai

_____ (not / win) the Nobel Peace Prize,

_____

_____

a antibiotics (not / be) developed.

b a documentary (not / be) made about her work.

c millions of people (die) from infections.

d most of them (be) killed.

e personal computers (not / become) so popular.

f she (not / be) murdered.

g social networking (not / be) possible.

h millions of trees (not / be) planted.

1 Tim Berners-Lee was an English engineer and computer scientist. He invented the World Wide Web in 1989, and the general public started using it in 1991. The information age grew because of the World Wide Web, and many people started using personal computers. Now, we can use the World Wide Web for social networking, like Facebook or Twitter.

2 Alexander Fleming was a physician who discovered penicillin in 1928. It was used to develop medicine that reduced the effects of infections. Penicillin was also very helpful in treating the wounded during World War II.

3 Dian Fossey was a conservationist who studied groups of mountain gorillas in Rwanda. She was very active in opposing poaching and worked toward saving gorilla habitats. She was murdered in her cabin in 1985, and it is believed that her murder was connected to her conservation work.

4 Wangari Maathai created the Green Belt Movement that focuses on environmental conservation. She encouraged the women of Kenya to plant trees throughout the country, and even paid the women a small amount of money for each tree they planted. A 2016 documentary talked about her work, for which she was awarded the Nobel Peace Prize.

2 Rewrite the pairs of sentences from Exercise 1. Use *if* in the middle of the sentences. You will need to change the position of some of the other words too.

1 _____

_____

_____

_____

2 _____

_____

_____

_____

3 _____

_____

_____

_____

4 _____

_____

_____

_____

3 Rewrite the sentences using the third conditional.

1 Tim Berners-Lee worked on hypertext because he wanted to share information with other researchers.

Tim _____

_____

2 Alexander Fleming didn't clean his dishes and so penicillin grew on them.

If _____

_____

3 Dian Fossey first went to Africa after a friend invited her on a safari.

Dian _____

_____

4 After Wangari Maathai started the Green Belt Movement, millions of trees were planted.

If _____

_____

Listening what if ... ?

4 ▶ **74** Listen to excerpts from four conversations. Complete the notes.

	Who?	Topic?
1	two work colleagues	
2	two friends	
3	father and son	
4	two friends	

poacher (n) /ˈpoʊtʃər/ an illegal hunter
authorities (n) /ɔːˈθɒrɪtiz/ official institutions or people in power
upset (v) /ʌpˈset/ to make someone unhappy or angry

5 ▶ **74** Listen again. Circle the correct option (a or b) according to the information in the conversations.

1 If the man hadn't taken the tablets,
  a he wouldn't have gotten better.
  b he would feel better now.

2 If Fleming hadn't discovered penicillin,
  a nobody else would have discovered it.
  b someone else would have discovered it.

3 Over 51 million trees wouldn't have been planted
  a if Wandari Maathai hadn't started the Green Belt Movement.
  b if Wandari Maathai hadn't gotten the government's help.

4 Wandari Maathai wouldn't have won a Nobel Prize
  a if she hadn't lived in Kenya.
  b if it hadn't been for her work in conservation.

5 The father couldn't find the website because
  a he'd missed some of the characters.
  b he'd typed in too many characters.

6 The son told his father
  a he could have Googled the site.
  b he should have called him for help.

7 According to the movie,
  a Dian Fossey was killed by poachers.
  b Dian Fossey and the poachers didn't get along.

8 Dian Fossey was
  a in favor of wildlife tourism.
  b against wildlife tourism.

6 **Dictation** **Scott of the Antarctic**

▶ **75** Listen and write the information about this photo, taken on Captain Scott's failed expedition to the South Pole in 1912. When you hear "period" this means you have reached the end of a sentence.

1 _____
_____

2 _____
_____

3 _____
_____

4 _____
_____

5 _____
_____

6 _____
_____

Reading a conflict in Cambodia

1 Read the article about Tuy Sereivathana. Match the excerpts (a–e) with the gaps in the text (1–5).

a They were essential in the construction of the Angkor Wat temple and are depicted in honor on its walls.

b The origins of his role are found in the difficulties that faced Cambodia after decades of political turmoil.

c The success of his project is unprecedented:

d When farmers were arrested for clearing the forest, they could no longer feed their families.

e An early demonstration of his team's commitment to remote communities was their role in the creation of schools.

2 Read the article, including the excerpts, again and find this information.

1 three reasons why the human–elephant conflict began

_____

_____

_____

2 one example of the elephant's historic role in Cambodia

_____

3 two problems that concerned farmers

_____

_____

A man of many talents

Tuy Sereivathana is a man with an unusual job title: Manager of the Human–Elephant Conflict Team for the Cambodian Elephant Conservation Group, for conservation group Fauna & Flora International. As a result of his expertise, not only the elephants but also 30,000 local people have benefited from the group's work. [1] _____

As masses of people relocated throughout Cambodia, they often created communities and farmland that affected elephant habitat. At the same time, with rain forests shrinking, hungry elephants came onto farmland, destroying crops. Desperately poor farmers fought back, killing elephants to protect their land and livelihood. As a result, Cambodia's elephant population, which numbered around 2,000 in 1995, crashed to several hundred. The action against the elephants was unexpected: they had been an integral part of Cambodia's traditions for centuries. [2] _____

To deal with the crisis, efforts at elephant conservation began. Given the historic status of the elephant, it was logical to expect progress in rekindling the connection between people and the environment. However, initial efforts didn't take the local people's needs into account sufficiently. Local people only associated wildlife protection with law enforcement. [3] _____ At this point, in 2003, Sereivathana became involved.

Day by day Sereivathana showed that he was concerned not only with elephants but also with human beings. [4] _____ The government had still not established schools in these areas and farmers were very concerned that their children could not read or write. Sereivathana helped set up schools and attract teachers, and made wildlife conservation part of the curriculum. After gaining local trust, he launched a series of low-cost, highly ingenious strategies for keeping both crops and elephants safe. [5] _____ since 2005, not a single wild elephant has been killed in Cambodia due to human conflict.

3 Circle the option or options (a–c) that are correct.

1 Tuy Sereivathana is an expert in _____.
  a conservation
  b elephants
  c history

2 Sereivathana's project has benefited _____.
  a animals
  b local politicians
  c people

3 The article shows that Sereivathana _____.
  a is a good teacher
  b is effective in complex situations
  c understands the place of conservation

4 Sereivathana's success is the result of _____.
  a gaining people's trust
  b innovative ideas
  c spending lots of money

5 The number of Cambodian elephants today has _____.
  a increased greatly
  b reached previous levels
  c stopped declining

Grammar *should have* and *could have*

4 Write sentences with *should (not) have* or *could (not) have*.

1 Cambodia's elephants / die out / completely.
  _____
  _____

2 In theory, / the conflict between people and elephants / happen.
  _____
  _____

3 The Cambodians / build / Angkor Wat without using elephants.
  _____
  _____

4 Conservation efforts / re-establish / respect for elephants.
  _____
  _____

5 Conservationists / pay / more attention to human needs.
  _____
  _____

6 The government / provide / schools.
  _____
  _____

5 Write a response to each comment. Use *should (not) have* or *could (not) have*.

1 I failed my exam!
  _____
  (study harder)

2 I left my front door unlocked!
  _____
  (someone / break in)

3 My brother's got malaria.
  _____
  (take / tablets)

4 This shirt doesn't fit.
  _____
  (buy / bigger)

5 My sister has been a great help.
  _____
  (we / do / without)

6 We got lost on the way.
  _____
  (use / GPS)

6 Pronunciation *should have* and *could have*

▶ 76 Listen and repeat the responses from Exercise 5.

12c Expert animals

Listening expert animals

1 Look at the photo. Circle the animals you see.
a   an octopus   b   a shrimp   c   a squid

2 ▶ 77 Listen to a podcast about expert animals. Check your answers to Exercise 1. Make notes on the following information.

1   two examples of animals that are expert hunters
   _____ , _____

2   two examples of animals that are experts at camouflage
   _____ , _____

3   something the octopus does when a predator sees it
   _____

4   what happened to the shrimp in the jar
   _____

5   what happened to the fish in a Seattle laboratory
   _____

6   how the Seattle laboratory staff discovered what had happened
   _____

---

ink (n) /ɪŋk/ a dark liquid, named after writing ink, that some animals produce
lid (n) /lɪd/ a cover for a container
mimic (v) /ˈmɪmɪk/ to copy or imitate the appearance of something
squirt (v) /skwərt/ to quickly force a liquid out of a container
trail (n) /treɪl/ a line or path of marks on the ground or floor

---

Word focus *go*

3 Look at these excerpts with *go* (1–3) from the podcast. Circle the correct meaning (a–c).

1   **going to** the other tanks
   a   disappearing   b   looking at   c   moving

2   **going back** to its own tank
   a   belonging   b   originating   c   returning

3   what was **going on**
   a   continuing   b   happening   c   talking

4 Complete the sentences with these words.

away	back	crazy	hungry
out	surfing	to	on

1   We live near the beach, so we go _____ every weekend.

2   Sorry, I didn't mean to interrupt. Please go _____—I'm listening.

3   What a mess I made! My boss will go _____ when she sees this.

4   Do you ever go _____ zoos?

5   These traditions go _____ generations.

6   If we can't find any restaurants open, we'll have to go _____ .

7   Are you going _____ this summer?

8   I'm not going _____ tonight—there's a great movie on TV.

5 Complete the sentences with these expressions.

go for a pizza	going out for a coffee
go for a run	going for a walk
go for a swim	gone out for lunch

1   I have a headache. I'm _____ to get some fresh air.

2   "Is Jim there?" "No, he's _____ . He'll be back in an hour."

3   Do you feel like _____ after this?

4   When I'm training for the marathon, I _____ every morning.

5   I don't have time to _____ today. The pool closes in twenty minutes.

6   "Are you doing anything special tonight?" "I think we'll just _____ ."

12d I'm so sorry!

Real life making and accepting apologies

1 Complete the sentences with these words. Then write MA for making an apology and AA for accepting an apology.

accident	help	things	trouble

1 I couldn't _____ it. ____
2 It's just one of those _____ ! ____
3 I'm really sorry you've gone to all this _____ . ____
4 Don't worry. It was an _____ . ____

2 Match the statements (1–6) with the responses (a–f).

1 You forgot to call me! ____
2 There's no paper in the photocopier. ____
3 I'm so sorry. I haven't had time to get you a gift. ____
4 I'm sorry, but I think I left your umbrella on the bus. ____
5 We've run out of bread. ____
6 I can't believe I dropped that! I'm really sorry. ____

a Don't blame me. I don't do the shopping.
b Don't worry about it. It was just an old one.
c It's my fault. I forgot to refill it. I'll do it now.
d It's not your fault. It could have happened to anyone.
e Oh, yes. Sorry about that!
f There's no need to apologize. It's not a problem.

3 Pronunciation sentence stress

▶ 78 Listen and repeat the exchanges from Exercise 2. Pay attention to the words you stress.

4 Grammar extra *not only … but also*

> ▶ **NOT ONLY … BUT ALSO**
>
> We use the structure *not only … but also* to add emphasis. The verb following *not only* is used with the auxiliary verb and the infinitive. The subject of the second verb goes between *but* and *also*.
>
> *Not only did he forget to buy the bread, but he also blamed me!* (= He forgot to buy the bread. He blamed me.)

Rewrite the sentences as one sentence. Use *not only … but also.*

1 You forgot to call me. You turned off your phone.
   _____
   _____

2 She lost my umbrella. She forgot to tell me.
   _____
   _____

3 He broke my vase. He didn't apologize.
   _____
   _____

4 They arrived late. They brought uninvited guests.
   _____
   _____

5 The octopus worked out how to get into the jar. It ate the shrimp.
   _____
   _____

5 Listen and respond making and accepting apologies

▶ 79 Listen to each comment. Respond with your own words. Then compare your response with the model answer that follows.

> *You forgot to text me!*

> *Oh, yes. Sorry about that!*

12e How to behave ...

Writing a website article

1 Writing skill checking your writing

a Look at the underlined mistakes in these sentences. What types of mistakes are they? Write the type of mistake with the sentence.

grammar	linking words	relevance
spelling	style	vocabulary

1 Here are some <u>images</u> of my <u>travel</u> to Brazil.

_____

2 My nephew is in Toronto this week. <u>My nephew</u> is learning English. <u>My nephew's</u> host family also speaks French.

_____

3 I've been to Mexico several times, <u>therefore</u> I've never learned Spanish.

_____

4 If I hadn't learned Italian at school, I <u>had never gone</u> on vacation to Rome.

_____

5 We used to go to Chicago every year and stay with the same <u>familys</u>.

_____

6 I went on a couple of homestays when I was a student. <u>I don't like flying</u>.

_____

b Correct the underlined mistakes in sentences 1–5 from Exercise 1a.

1 _____
2 _____
3 _____
4 _____
5 _____

2 You are writing an article for a website that arranges host families for foreign language students in the United States. The purpose of the article is to give advice to families who want to be hosts. Read quickly through the sections (a–h) and decide which is the introduction. Ignore the numbers in parentheses for the moment.

a And finally, be patient with them when they speak English. If you never try to learn a language yourself, you try taking a short course so that you know how it feels! (2)

b Find out if there is anything your student can't eat, either for religious reasons or because they dislike a particular food item or plate. I don't like eggs, for example. (2)

c Make sure that you explain your household and family rules very clearly at the begginning. (1)

d Respect their privacy in spite of they are in your home. For the duration of their stay, their bedroom is there own private space. (2)

e Talk to your student about life in the student's own country. This helps you to anticipate what problems the student might have during the student's visit. (3)

f Treat the student as you would expect your own child to be treated if they are abroad. (1)

g We've had quite a few foreign students stay since the last few years, and each time it was been an enjoyable experience. If you're thinking about becoming a host family, here are a few tips for you. (2)

h You can ask your student to help with things as setting the table if that's what your own children do, but don't expect them to help you with the homework. (2)

3 Check each section using the criteria in Exercise 1. The number of mistakes in each section is given in parentheses. Underline the mistakes.

4 Correct the mistakes and put the sections in a logical order. (More than one order is possible.) Write the finished article: *Tips for host families*.

Wordbuilding prefix *in-*, *un-*, *im-*

> ► **WORDBUILDING prefix *in-*, *un-*, *im-***
>
> We can add *in-* and *-un* to the beginning of some adjectives to mean "not." We can also use *im-* before some adjectives that begin with the letter *p*.
> *an inappropriate place, an unexpected experience, it was impossible.*

1 Add *in-*, *un-*, or *im-* to the beginning of these words.

1	_____accurate	8	_____necessary
2	_____conclusive	9	_____offensive
3	_____credible	10	_____patient
4	_____effective	11	_____polite
5	_____efficient	12	_____possible
6	_____expected	13	_____tolerant
7	_____expensive	14	_____true

2 Circle the correct option (a–c).

1 A lot of things you read online are actually **lies**.
   a ineffective
   b intolerant
   c untrue

2 The hotel receptionist was **no good at his job**. He couldn't even find our room key!
   a inaccurate
   b inefficient
   c impossible

3 Wow! Sue quit her job. That was **sudden!**
   a incredible
   b inexpensive
   c unexpected

4 There is some evidence to support the theory, but it's **not certain**.
   a inconclusive
   b inefficient
   c impossible

5 You should never be **rude** to your host.
   a impatient
   b impolite
   c impossible

6 I don't think the hotel had to apologize. It was**n't needed**.
   a inaccurate
   b impatient
   c unnecessary

Learning skills dealing with exams

3 Try this quiz to see if you're an expert when it comes to exams. Circle the options (a–c) you think are correct.

1 What will help you get good grades on an exam?
   a knowing the format of the exam
   b timing yourself for each question
   c studying vocabulary and grammar from the course

2 What should you do to prepare for an exam?
   a do some practice papers
   b go on vacation to an English-speaking country
   c look through your notebook

3 How should you behave during an exam?
   a try to finish as quickly as possible
   b leave some time to check your answers
   c spend more time on the questions with high points

> **Answers**
> 1 All of these are good strategies.
> 2 Option b is not really necessary, although it might be a nice thing to do when your exams are over!
> 3 Option a is not a good idea at all! Use your time well.

Check!

4 Write the names of the things in the grid. The letters in the shaded squares spell a kind of expert who would be useful on a field trip to see wildlife.

1

2

3

4

5

6

7

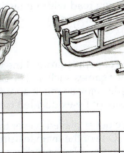

1					
2					
3					
4					
5					
6					
7					

Audioscripts

Unit 1

▶ 01

OK. then. As usual on Friday's show, we are asking you at home a question. This week our question was about your idea of national identity—when do you feel American? Let's start with some of your replies you sent by email.

This one is from Jeff in Chicago. He says, "Every time I go to a baseball game. Americans love baseball. People say it's our national sport. I believe it."

Now here's one from Maggie, in Dallas. She says, "I feel American when I eat fast food. Actually, I'm eating a cheeseburger and French fries right now!"

That's interesting, Maggie! Now you're making me hungry. Did you see the story about fast food in the news last week? More people are eating fast food now than ever before. Some schools are even serving it. That seems like a bad idea to me.

Now here's an interesting email, from Paulo. He says, "I'm not American, I'm Brazilian, but I'm living in Los Angeles now. I feel American when I go to the movies here. The theaters are huge, and they play Hollywood blockbusters all the time. I watched American movies in Brazil, but seeing them here feels different."

Here's an email from Ali. He came to the U.S. from Egypt, when he was a child. He feels American when he uses slang. He says, "I love to use words like 'cool,' 'awesome,' and 'chill.'"

OK, we have time for one more reply before we take a break for the news. Lisa says, "Hi! I'm listening to your show from our car. My family is on a road trip, which feels like a very American thing to do. We go to a different place every year. We're driving across the country on the famous Route 66. We started in Illinois and drove through Missouri, Oklahoma, Texas, New Mexico, and Arizona. We are now at the end of the route in California. I'm looking at some beautiful palm trees."

Ah, Lisa! That sounds … well … awesome! I'm sitting here looking at a gray studio wall. OK, coming up to ten o'clock, here's the news.

▶ 04

1   Do you taste the words you hear?
2   Do words have color for you?
3   Can you read without tasting words?
4   Which senses do you mix up?

▶ 05

Millions of people around the world regularly play computer games such as The Sims or Dragon Quest. What do people enjoy so much about these games? A team at the University of Essex decided to try and find out.

If you've never played one of these games, then let me explain. One of the main features of many video games is that when you play, you choose a new identity. The game identity can be one which is a real-world character, such as in The Sims game, or it can be a powerful superhero character.

Now you might think that turning into a different character is a way of escaping or running away from your everyday life. But the university team discovered that this isn't really what is going on. It seems that players often choose a character that is a little bit similar to their own personalities. They enjoy the game more when this is the case, compared to times when their game identity is very different to themselves. So video games mean that people can think about the kind of person they want to be in a "perfect world," and then they can play the role of that kind of person.

The results of the university team's studies are interesting because we often read negative things about video games—that they are dangerous or addictive. It turns out that, in fact, they increase people's happiness and positive feelings about themselves.

▶ 09

1   A: Hello, how are you? My name's Grace Larsen.
    B: I'm very pleased to meet you. I'm Alberto Costa.
2   C: I work in marketing. What about you?
    D: I'm in IT, actually.
3   E: I'm the manager of Pink Cosmetics.
    F: Oh yes, I know that company very well.
4   G: I'm looking for a new job at the moment, actually.
    H: Are you? What kind of thing are you looking for?
5   I: How about meeting again?
    J: Yes, let me give you my card.

Unit 2

▶ 11

R = Robin, J = Judy
R: Have you heard of this guy, Philippe Petit?
J: No, I don't think so. Who is he?
R: He's done some amazing things—he walks on tightropes.
J: Is he a circus performer? I don't really enjoy circuses.
R: No, he's not in a circus or anything. He's a … um a high-wire artist. He's done high-wire walks in some amazing places.
J: What kind of places?
R: Well, he's walked—on a wire—across the towers of Notre Dame and also the Sydney Harbour Bridge. His most famous walk was in 1974. He crossed from one tower to the other, at the twin towers of the World Trade Center in New York.
J: Wow! I wonder what that felt like?
R: I know! How scary!
J: But how did he balance on a wire in the middle of … nothing! How wide was the wire?
R: I don't know. Does it matter? Even if it was a meter wide, it's still a really difficult thing to do.
J: And how high up was he?
R: It says here 139 meters.
J: That's crazy! He was lucky not to fall off.
R: I don't think it was luck. I think it was experience. He decided to do the New York walk in 1968. And his first walk was in Paris in 1971. So it actually took six years to plan the New York one.
J: Six years?
R: Yeah. And then, when he did it, he didn't have permission. The newspapers at the time called it "the artistic crime of the century." He was on the wire for 45 minutes—he went back and forth eight times! Eight! And when the people on the ground noticed him, he started dancing.
J: Unbelievable!

R: Anyway, they've made a movie about him. It's on tonight. Should we watch it?

▶ 13
1 Performing in public makes me nervous.
2 I enjoy being in the spotlight.
3 I've never given a speech in my life.
4 Going to dances is a good way of meeting people.
5 Telling jokes is very hard to do.
6 I've been on stage a couple of times.

▶ 14
The experimental movie *Life in a Day* is an unusual kind of film—in fact, it's possibly unique. It gives us a picture of life in our world—the whole world—on one single day: July 24, 2010. The movie is a documentary—not a drama, a thriller, or a romantic comedy. But at the same time, it has moments of drama and of romance. In fact, the movie is simply a lot of moments—90 minutes of moments from people's lives around the world on that July 24th. Some of these moments are connected, some aren't. At times during these 90 minutes, it's difficult to concentrate, to be honest. Watching it becomes almost exhausting. So many images flash in front of your eyes. But the idea of the movie is certainly interesting. The movie itself is made from videos shot by ordinary people. There are no actors, professional filmmakers, or special effects. And although there is no story, there are themes: love, fear, hope, and so on.

The project began when movie director Kevin Macdonald had an idea: "to take the temperature of the planet on a single day," as he puts it. He sent about 400 cameras to 40 countries and asked people three questions: "What do you love? What do you fear? What do you have in your pocket?" Then people used the cameras to film their lives, or the lives of those around them, and sent the footage back to Macdonald. And the astonishing thing was that the project grew to be much bigger than 400 people with cameras. A week after the "day," Macdonald and his team had 4,500 hours of footage in 81,000 video clips from 192 countries. Even more astonishing, perhaps, was the fact that at that stage, Macdonald didn't have a plan for his movie. He wanted to see all the footage first and try to choose 90 minutes from that.

So, what did he choose? What kind of picture do we get? There are women in Ghana singing while they work, an English student having a drink with his dad, men in India gossiping, market sellers in the Philippines having lunch, people doing something kind for a neighbor … the list goes on. And there are words to go with the images too. The faces speak to us, telling us that they "love soccer" or are afraid of "growing up." The movie has been pretty successful—perhaps more than Macdonald expected. If you've missed it in the theater, you can watch it on YouTube. It's an interesting way to spend an hour and a half.

▶ 16
1 Q: Do you feel like going to the theater on Friday night?
  R: Yeah, why not?
2 Q: Do you want to go out tonight?
  R: Yes, sure.

3 Q: There's a circus in town. Do you like the sound of that?
  R: It doesn't really appeal to me.
4 Q: What did you think of the movie?
  R: It was absolutely incredible.
5 Q: Did you enjoy the performance?
  R: To be honest, I was really bored.
6 Q: What was the concert like?
  R: It was the best concert I've ever been to.

Unit 3

▶ 18
Hurricanes are giant, wet, and windy tropical storms. They bring winds of over 250 kilometers an hour, and hurricane clouds can carry enough water for more than nine trillion liters of rainfall in a day. Now, if you're thinking that you don't know the difference between hurricanes, cyclones, and typhoons, don't worry. They are actually the same thing. The different names just come from the different parts of the world—cyclones start in the Indian Ocean and typhoons in the western Pacific Ocean. Hurricanes begin in the Atlantic Ocean where their annual season is from mid-August to late October.

One of the wettest and most destructive hurricanes in recent history was Hurricane Mitch. It hit the Caribbean and Central America in November 1998. By the time Mitch reached the coast, most people had already left the area. When the danger had passed, and people had returned home, they couldn't believe what had happened. In Honduras, farmland had turned into desert. Bridges and roads had disappeared. Rivers had changed course. As Mitch passed over Honduras, so much rain fell that some rivers flooded to six times their normal size. In one day, the area had the equivalent of 200 days of rainfall. In places where there had been rivers with lines of trees, now there was nothing. The trees had all washed away. This kind of thing is not so unusual during hurricanes, but the power of Mitch was extreme. The tremendous winds had picked up sand and carried it for many kilometers before dropping it in a new area. Suddenly, there was a desert where people had had farms. Mitch had completely changed the land and, of course, the lives of the people who lived there. It took them many years to recover.

And, although there will be hurricanes in the future as powerful as Mitch, the World Meteorological Organization decided the name Mitch will never be used again.

▶ 19
a Both men are now in the hospital.
b The men had fallen out of their boat.
c Their families had called the Coast Guard.
d The Coast Guard rescued two men from the sea this weekend.
e The men hadn't returned from a fishing trip.

▶ 20
I = interviewer, P = Pauline
I: Now, you may remember seeing the name Bundanoon in the news headlines a while ago. Bundanoon is a small town near Sydney, Australia. It has its own supply of water from an underground water reserve.

Some years ago, the residents of the town discovered that a water company had applied for permission to extract this water, bottle it, and sell it as drinking water. We spoke to Bundanoon resident Pauline Tiller earlier this week, about what happened next. Pauline, why didn't you want this water company to go ahead with their plans?

P: Basically, because we were drinking the water in our homes, direct from our taps. We didn't want to buy bottled water—especially when it was already our own town's water supply!

I: And how did you get involved in the story?

P: Well, I was using an old newspaper to mop up a water leak one morning when something in the paper caught my attention. I stopped and read this astonishing letter Huw Kingston had written about banning bottled water.

I: Huw Kingston is a local businessman in Bundanoon, is that right?

P: Yes, he had come up with this revolutionary idea—he wanted the town to fight the water company. And he also wanted us to ban bottled water completely! As soon as I read his letter, I knew that was the answer!

I: And what did you do next?

P: A few residents got together to investigate how we could go "bottled-water free." At that time, we didn't know we were pioneers! While we were looking for information, we heard about another Australian town that had gone "plastic-bag free." This really encouraged and inspired us. Then we found out that the carbon footprint of bottled water is 300 times greater than tap water! It became obvious that bottled water is a crazy idea. So we had a town meeting to discuss the whole thing and the town decided to become bottled-water free.

I: And I believe journalists from a national newspaper arrived while you were holding the meeting?

P: Yes, a lot of national and international newspapers had heard about our story. After they wrote about us, we got a lot of support from environmental movements. And in September 2009, we became the first bottled-water free town in Australia.

I: So you banned bottled water. But now, what do people—visitors to the town, for example—do if they want to get a drink of water?

P: All the water in our town is free, so you can get it from the tap. And if you want to take some water with you, our shops sell our own "Bundanoon" reusable bottles.

▶ 21

1 We were fishing on the lake.
2 I was trying to bring the fish in.
3 He was shouting at me.
4 We were sitting in the boat.

▶ 22

1 Q: Did I ever tell you about the time we ran out of gas?
   R: No. Where were you going?
2 S: I remember when I broke my leg.
   R: When did that happen?
3 S: I almost had a car accident last night.
   R: Really? What happened?
4 S: A couple of months ago, I decided to leave my job.
   R: Oh? Why?
5 S: You'll never believe who we saw in town last weekend!
   R: Oh? Who was it?
6 Q: Did I tell you what I was doing when you called?
   R: No. What were you doing?

Unit 4

▶ 23

1 I look at my new son and I wonder about his future. The world will be a very different place in a few years' time, I'm sure of that. I want his life to be better than mine, but I worry that it might not be. There are some things I'm sure about: he'll learn to use a computer before he goes to school and he won't leave school at sixteen like I did. But everything is changing so quickly—it's really hard to say what his life will be like.

2 I think my baby will have a great life. Robots and computers will take care of all the routine, boring things like shopping, housework, and stuff, so she'll have lots of time to enjoy herself. She'll probably drive an electric car and live in a house that recycles everything. She might work from home, but she definitely won't work full time like I do. It'll be great!

3 My baby will definitely live longer than me. She'll probably live to be a hundred—that's what they say about babies born today. Will she be healthy? I think so—there are so many advances in medicine these days. I think they'll certainly find cures for many of the health problems we face today. So she might get sick at some point in her life, but they'll be able to cure her.

4 When I think about my children's future, the thing that worries me most is the situation with the environment—things like climate change and oil and gas running out really concern me. This could affect their world in ways we haven't imagined. It seems that my kids will probably speak Chinese—at least that's what people keep telling me! They may not learn it at school, but they'll need it for work and business, I suppose. So that could be a challenge!

▶ 24

1 People won't get sick in the future.
2 School students may study from home.
3 Climate change could affect everybody.
4 People will probably travel less in the future.
5 People might work until the age of 75.
6 English will probably be the only language you need.

▶ 25

1 It's ten miles from here.
2 Send me an email.
3 I'll see you soon.
4 I hope I don't fail this exam.
5 There's no oil in this jar.
6 How do you feel?

▶ 26

H = host, I = interviewer, A = Anton, C = Carey

H: Well, that's about all for today, but in our next program, we'll meet some of the "internet generation"—people who grew up with the internet. We'll find out what it means to be 21 today and if it's so different from past generations. What's life like for this generation, and how do they view what's ahead? Here's a little taste of next week's program …

A: I don't believe in making plans. Plans are for old people. I like to be spontaneous.

I: So, marriage … a family … a home of your own?

A: Yeah, when I'm older! Say … thirty-something. First, I'm going to enjoy myself.

I: You don't want to settle down, then? But you have a good job.

A: Oh yeah, work is fine, and I'll probably be promoted soon. I work hard, earn a good salary. And I like to spend it!

I: So Carey, what are you planning now that you've graduated?

C: Well, in July we have my graduation ceremony, my 21st birthday, and my parents' 25th wedding anniversary in the same week, so that's going to be amazing. We're all really looking forward to that. Then after that, my main aim is to get a full-time job—because at the moment I still have the part-time job I've had since I was at school.

I: Does that worry you?

C: Worry me? No. Something will come along, for sure. I'll try anything … I believe you have to go through life with an open mind, or you might miss an opportunity.

H: That was the voice of Carey, who in fact was in a car accident at 16 and has been in a wheelchair ever since. And before that you heard Anton, a young man who has also had some challenges in his life. Just two of the people you can hear more from in next week's program, *Turning 21*, which will explore the hopes and dreams of the internet generation. We hope you can join us then. And we hope you will be inspired, like we were, by what you hear.

▶ 28

1 Q: Are you going to fill in the form?
  A: Yes, I am.
2 Q: Will you be OK?
  A: Yes, I'm sure I will.
3 Q: Does she speak English?
  A: Yes, I think she does.
4 Q: Will they call you today?
  A: No, I don't think they will.

▶ 29

1 Q: Are you looking for a new job at the moment?
  R: Yes, I am actually.
2 Q: Can you help me fill in this application form?
  R: Yes, sure.
3 Q: Do you mind if I give your name as a reference?
  R: No, of course not.
4 Q: Have you finished your resume yet?
  R: Yes, I think so.
5 Q: Could you show me how to upload my resume?
  R: Sure, no problem.
6 Q: Can you come to an interview next week?
  R: Yes, of course.

Unit 5

▶ 30

W: What are you looking at? Oh, recipes! Are you going to make something?

M: Yes, I've invited some friends over for dinner on Saturday, but I can't decide what to cook.

W: Are they close friends?

M: Well, yes, but why do you ask?

W: Because it will help you make up your mind. If they're good friends, then it's their company that's important, so maybe it doesn't matter what you cook.

M: That's a good point. But even though they're close friends, I still want to make them a nice meal. So I'm thinking, I could make cheese soufflé … or prawn curry … or just a simple steak?

W: A cheese soufflé is really difficult, isn't it? Can I make a suggestion?

M: Of course!

W: Make something you can prepare in advance. Then you won't have to spend so much time in the kitchen when they arrive.

M: Another good point! Anyway, all this talk about food is making me hungry! Do you want to get a sandwich?

▶ 31

Welcome back. You're listening to KLH radio. We heard about the movie *Australia* earlier in the program. Well, I've just come back from a trip to Australia, and one of the places I visited was Kakadu National Park, near Darwin up in the north. The park is run by the government and the traditional Aboriginal owners, and it's in a beautiful area. Visitors are only allowed to go into certain parts of the park, and for some trips you have to go with a guide.

I met an Aboriginal woman there who takes tourists into the Outback and shows them how to survive on the food you can find there. They call this food "bush tucker." Well, standing in the park with the Aboriginal guide, I looked around me and to be honest I couldn't see that there was that much to eat. There were a few trees and a lot of grass—but it was dry, brown grass, and there wasn't much else. Then the Aboriginal woman waded into a watering hole, which I thought was taking a risk because of the crocodiles. There are crocodile warning signs all through the area saying you shouldn't do that. But I later found out that the Aborigines sometimes eat the younger small crocodiles. And they also collect crocodile eggs.

So, from the watering hole she collected some water lilies. The stalks were like celery, so we chewed on them and that was OK. And they had these little balls attached which we also ate. So far, so good. Then she dug up some grass and we ate part of the roots—they call them bush carrots.

Then she showed us a tree and said it was a good cure for sore throats, colds, and headaches. She pulled a handful of leaves off the tree and in the bundle of leaves there was an ants' nest. She took a handful of ants and started to crush them quickly in her hand. I think you have to do this quickly because the ants bite. So we ate them—the crushed ants—too. They had a lemon flavor—it was the best thing we ate that day. Really, we had a complete dinner right there from what had appeared to be nothing at all! I don't think you should do this without a guide, though.

▶ 32

2 You have to picnic in designated areas.
5 You have to contact the warden in advance of your visit.
6 You don't have to show identification to enter.
8 You have to report any incidents with wild animals.

▶ 33

1 If you go to the gym,
2 You'll feel better
3 You won't lose weight
4 I'll tell you about my diet

a when I see you.
b you'll get fit.
c unless you give up junk food.
d if you change your diet.

▶ 34

In today's show, we hear about two people who decided to try and get away from the 24-hour lifestyle and so-called rat race of modern life. The first by traveling to a different culture, the second by radically changing his way of life without leaving his own culture. What did their experiences teach them? How easy is it—or is it even possible—to break out of the restrictions and expectations of modern society?

So first, radio journalist Lisa Napoli. She was on a search for meaning in her life when someone suggested she head to Bhutan. No 1960s-style hippy traveler, Napoli actually went to Bhutan with a high-profile job—to help in the setting up of a new radio station. She fell in love with the country and recently wrote a book titled *Radio Shangri-La: What I Learned in Bhutan, the Happiest Kingdom on Earth*. In her book, Napoli describes how learning to live with less made her life richer. She explains that in Bhutan it was impossible to live a frenetic 24/7 lifestyle. So many people think they need and enjoy having a lot of stuff, but what if that's not possible? For Napoli, the key is to appreciate what is around you rather than to constantly desire and strive for things you do not have. If we value simplicity and respect the natural environment, we will be more content, she feels.

But how quickly can we adapt to a different culture in this way? Napoli found that for her it was easy. What about attempting to live in a different way within your own culture? There must be so much pressure to conform to what is around you. How determined do you have to be to ignore that? One person who knows is a man named Mark Boyle. He decided to give up using money for a year. How did he manage? He soon discovered if you want to live with no money, you will need a lot more time. Even routine tasks such as washing clothes takes a couple of hours instead of just thirty minutes in a washing machine. He had to cycle everywhere as he had no money to get the bus or train—but on the other hand, he didn't need to pay for an expensive gym membership any more. Perhaps the most valuable lesson that Mark Boyle learned was the value of friendship, community, and relationships based on trust not money.

So if you *are* fed up with the modern pace of life, how realistic is it to make changes like this? Maybe you don't need to be so radical—there are other ways of slowing down that might be just as effective. You won't know unless you try.

▶ 35
1 Are you comfortable at this table?
2 Good evening. Do you have a reservation?
3 They're a national chain.
4 It's hard to eat well when you're traveling.

▶ 37
1 Q: Are you ready to order?
  R: Not quite. We just need a minute.
2 Q: Would you like something to drink?
  R: Yes, I'll have a bottle of sparkling water, please.
3 Q: And for your main course?
  R: I'll have the cod.
4 Q: Would you like to see the dessert menu?
  R: No, thanks. We'll just have coffee.
5 Q: Did you enjoy your meal?
  R: Yes, it was all delicious, thanks.

Unit 6

▶ 38
There are a few things that everyone seems to recognize as typically American—tipping, baseball, and waiting in line for example. In the U.S., we learn how to wait patiently in a line from the very first day we go to elementary school. And then we line up everywhere—waiting for a bus, waiting in a store, waiting to buy tickets, and so on. To us, the system seems obvious. The person who arrives first is the first one to get on the bus, to be served in the store, or to get the tickets. But you don't find lining up in every culture. And now, researchers in Denmark say that sometimes, if you serve the last person in the line first, the line moves more quickly. Yes, that's right, the person who arrives last should be served first. I know what you're thinking: "How can that possibly work?"

Well, I've had a close look at what the Danish researchers say. They point out that the problem with traditional lines is that people tend to arrive too early, then a line develops and everyone has to wait a long time. One example of a place where this system doesn't always apply is in airports. Usually, when you're waiting to find out which departure gate you have to go to, you spend time in the departure lounge. You can't start lining up at the gate because you only find out which number it is when it opens. The Danish study looked at several different situations like this airport example and found that people don't wait as long if the last person is served first. The reason for this is that people behave differently if this system is used. If you know that the people who arrive first don't always get served first, then there's no point in lining up early. So everyone arrives at different times and the lines aren't as long. The really important point here is that you have to know in advance that this is the system. And the system doesn't work in all situations—I really can't imagine what might happen at a bus stop if the last person to arrive got on the bus first, can you?

▶ 39
1 I think I may have seen it before.
2 It can't have been on before.
3 It must have been a trailer.
4 You might have been busy.
6 I suppose the people could have called by mistake.

▶ 40
1 She must have been in a hurry.
2 He might not have realized the time.
3 It might have been on a different channel.
4 They can't have forgotten.
5 He must have switched it off.

▶ 41
The strange and fascinating phenomenon of crop circles—which actually aren't simply circular, but form intricate geometric patterns in farm fields—has inspired many possible explanations over the years. Crop-circle enthusiasts who prefer paranormal explanations for the circles believe that they must be messages left behind by extraterrestrial visitors, while more conventionally scientific-minded people have theorized that they might have resulted from natural physical forces, such as wind or heat. But now, there's another, even more bizarre explanation: wallabies.

As BBC News and many other news outlets are reporting, Lara Giddings, Attorney General for the Australian state of Tasmania, told a Parliamentary hearing that wallabies have been eating poppies in fields that provide legal opium for morphine and other painkillers. Apparently, according to Giddings, the wallabies are eating the poppies and then becoming so disoriented that they run around in the fields erratically, creating paths that resemble crop circles.

An official with an Australian poppy-cultivation company told ABC News that in the process of consuming the poppy-seed capsules, the wallabies often also eat some of the substances that cause opium's hallucinogenic effect in humans. The weird suggestion that animals may have been the cause of Australian crop circles, however, doesn't really explain the crop-circle phenomenon. Are they capable of creating the sort of intricate geometric patterns seen in most crop circles? What about the crop circles found thousands of kilometers away from Australia, in the U.K.?

This odd explanation also doesn't account for the alternative view that crop circles are nothing more than elaborate jokes. A University of Oregon physicist, Richard Taylor, speculates that crop-circle hoaxers may now be using increasingly sophisticated tools such as GPS devices and laser pointers to burn complex patterns into fields.

▶ 43
1 S: Look! It's snowing outside.
   R: Are you sure?
2 S: I'm getting married.
   R: You're kidding me!
3 S: Someone in Siberia has seen a yeti.
   R: Come off it!
4 S: I read in the paper that there are no fish left in the sea.
   R: You must be joking!
5 S: The date on today's newspaper is 2025.
   R: They must have made a mistake.
6 S: From next year, the clocks change to ten-hour days.
   R: That can't be right!

▶ 44
1 Environmentalists in the Philippines have been helping frogs cross a road and get to a river safely for the last three years. During the month of October, a wildlife group in the north of the country monitors the road with the help of local students. The aim is to avoid frog deaths. Campaigners say that frogs are increasingly under threat as humans move into their habitat.
2 In Holland this month, an unusual new ice cream is going on sale. The main ingredient is camel's milk. The producers have used camel's milk because it has less fat and more vitamins than normal milk.

Unit 7

▶ 45
1 When I was little, I used to live with my grandparents.
2 Who did you use to live with?
3 I didn't use to like my school.
4 Did you use to enjoy going to school?
5 We didn't use to play outside very often.
6 Where did you use to play?

▶ 46
All great cities change over time. Timbuktu, in Mali, is an example of this. Timbuktu used to be a thriving city and an important place of learning for Islam. Centuries ago, it played a huge role in the spread of Islam in Africa. Even today, three important mosques still exist in Timbuktu, and Timbuktu is the home of one of the world's great collections of ancient manuscripts. The great teachings of Islam, from astronomy and mathematics to medicine and law, were collected and produced here in several hundred thousand manuscripts. This heritage is recognized by the inclusion of Timbuktu on the list of World Heritage Sites.

Timbuktu's geographical location was an important factor in its history. It was at the crossroads of major trading routes. The Niger River passes through Timbuktu on its 4,000-kilometer journey from Guinea in the west to the Niger delta in Nigeria. Camel trains used to pass through the city continuously on their way north and south. They would bring gold from the mining areas in the south and salt from the north. The river also used to bring cargoes of gold, as well as slaves, to the city. People from all of the major North African cities would come here to exchange horses and cloth for gold. Equally, scholars from places as far away as Cairo and Baghdad came to teach and study.

In the 16th century, Timbuktu was invaded by Moroccan forces. The scholars began to leave and the trade routes also started to move closer to the coast. The golden age of the city was over.

▶ 48
19.20.21 What is it? A simple sequence of numbers or something more meaningful than that? In fact, it's the name of a fascinating project about modern cities. The man responsible for this project is the architect Richard Saul Wurman. His project is about collecting information on 19 cities that will have more than 20 million people in the 21st century.

How and why did he get the idea for a project like this? What's it all about? In the year 2008, for the first time in history, there were more people living inside cities than outside them. This is one of the biggest changes in the way we live that we have ever seen. Wurman looked on the internet and tried to find the appropriate books and lists that would give him information—data, maps, and so on—so that he could understand why urban life is getting more and more popular. As he couldn't find what he was looking for, he decided to collect the data himself. And so the 19.20.21 project was born.

So, why do we move to cities? People are pulled toward cities because that's where they have greater opportunities. Cities are where you put museums, where you put universities, where you put the centers of government and business. The inventions, the discoveries, the music, and the art in our world all take place in these places where people come together.

The cities that the 19.20.21 project is looking at are those of extremes, the most obvious extreme being size. A thousand years ago, the biggest city was Cordoba in Spain. Three hundred years ago, it was Beijing—a century ago London, then New York City in 1950, and today it's Tokyo. But the fastest growing city today is Lagos, Nigeria. So the interesting cities are the ones that are clearly the largest, the oldest, the fastest growing (like Lagos), the most densely populated (that's Mumbai in India), or that cover the largest area, like Los Angeles.

If we want to make things better—not worse—in our cities, then we need to understand them. We need to be able to compare them. We have to understand before we act. And although there are a lot of little ideas for making things better—reduce traffic jams, increase safety, have cleaner air—you can't solve the problem with a collection of little ideas. So, the 19.20.21 project brings together the information we need.

▶ 49
1 Do you usually take the bus or walk?
2 Do you want to go out or stay in?
3 Do you prefer action movies or romances?
4 Would you prefer tea or coffee?

▶ 50

1 Q: Do you usually take the bus or walk?
   R: I prefer to walk because it's better for me.
2 Q: Do you want to go out or stay in?
   R: I'd rather go out. It's the weekend.
3 Q: Do you prefer action movies or romances?
   R: Romances. I find action movies kind of boring.
4 Q: Would you prefer tea or coffee?
   R: Tea, please. I've already had several cups of coffee today.

Unit 8

▶ 51

Boyd Matson is one of the greatest travel journalists of our time. I've been a big fan of his work for years. Listening to his radio shows or reading his articles, I feel as if I have been with him on his many adventures. I say "adventures" because Matson usually manages to find excitement on his trips. He's suffered dehydration, broken bones, snakebite, and a long list of other troubles. But he never seems to take these problems too seriously.

Matson had dreamed of traveling since he was a child. He read a book about Chinese political leaders and another about a missionary's experience in New Guinea, and he knew he wanted to go to China and New Guinea one day. As an adult working for NBC News, he spent half his time traveling and reporting from places that were in the news.

In a recent article, Matson talks about his most memorable experiences. One was visiting the Khumbu Icefall on Mount Everest. Although he was really excited to get there, it was an unhappy time—the best-known Sherpa climber in the world was killed during the trip. It was a reminder that travel is a lot of fun, but it can also be dangerous. You have to be careful not to take unnecessary risks in places like Everest.

Now that Matson has a family, he doesn't travel quite as often as before. But his children have helped him see things from a fresh angle. He gave one of them a camera and one a video camera, and said it was fun to compare their shots with his own. As for the future, Matson intends to go to new places with a different attitude—more as a participant than an observer. He describes his travel philosophy as "get off the tour bus." I can't wait to see where he goes next and to join him there from the comfort of my living room.

▶ 52

1 How long was your last vacation?
2 How long did it take to get to your destination?
3 How long have you been in this class?
4 How long have you been learning English?
5 How long have you spent on this unit?

▶ 53

H = host, S = Suzanne, A = Andrew Marshall,
M = Marco, J = Jane

H: OK, our lines are now open, so please call us with your travel queries. Our studio guest this morning is Andrew Marshall, an expert in all aspects of tourism. He's here to answer your questions. And our first caller is Suzanne … with a question about flying, I think. Hello?
S: Hi, yes, um I've been hearing a lot about low-cost airlines recently—about how they aren't as reliable as the big companies. I saw an article last week and it said that if you have problems like flight delays or your luggage goes missing, the budget airlines don't always look after

you very well. I've used low-cost airlines in the past, but I'm not sure about flying with them again now.
A: Hi, Suzanne. Yes, I've seen some of the reports that you talk about, too. But you don't need to worry. All airlines have to follow certain standards and guidelines—that's the budget companies as well as the big airlines. So, relax and book your budget flight!
H: And our next caller is Marco.
M: Hi, well, my parents have always gone on package vacations that they buy from a travel agent. But I think they can save money if they buy the travel tickets online directly from the airline and the hotel. They don't agree with me. Who's right?
A: Hello, Marco. This is a very interesting question, but it doesn't have a very simple answer, I'm afraid. It's true that more and more people are arranging the kinds of things that travel agents always used to do. But I think that the real reason for this is that it gives you flexibility, rather than it costing less. Of course, it depends on the type of vacation. Hotel rooms in big vacation resorts can be cheaper because the hotel sells big "blocks" to travel companies. If you book direct with the hotel, you might have to pay full price. I think an internet search is the best place to start—then you can compare prices with the package deals.
H: And Jane has a specific question about travel insurance.
J: Yes, I plan to visit Asia next year, but the thing is, the travel insurance seems really expensive. Do I really need it?
A: Hi, Jane. Yes, you do. But not just for Asia, for any foreign travel. Accidents can happen wherever you are. The things that can go wrong don't need to be dramatic—you might just get a really bad toothache in a place where dentists are pretty expensive. As far as I'm concerned, vacation insurance is the best thing you can spend your vacation money on.
H: Andrew, before we take the next call, let me ask you a bit more about insurance …

▶ 55

1 Q: Is something wrong?
   R: Yes, I lost my passport.
2 Q: I wonder if you could help us?
   R: Yes, of course. What's the problem?
3 Q: I'm sorry. Have you been waiting long?
   R: Yes, we've been here for ages.
4 Q: Is there anything you can do about the noise?
   R: I'll speak to the manager.
5 Q: Can I help you?
   R: Yes, I hope so. It's about our bags.

Unit 9

▶ 56

A: Do you have any ideas about a present for Aunt Jane yet?
B: Well, I know we want to buy something really special and unusual, but I haven't really had any good ideas so far.
A: Why don't we look on the internet? Type in "luxury gifts" or something like that and see what comes up.
B: OK … Let's see.
A: There, look—gold. You can't get more special than gold.
B: Do you think she'd like jewelry? She doesn't seem to wear it much—just earrings and a plain gold chain.
A: Well, maybe if we got something custom-made. It says here that items can be made to the customer's specification from a selection of designs.
B: Yeah, that's worth thinking about. What else is there?
A: Oh, click on that rug! I've always loved these hand-made rugs. What does it say about them?

106

B: "Our traditional hand-woven rugs are still being made today using the same techniques and quality materials as hundreds of years ago … these classic designs have not been altered for centuries … and are imported direct from the producer … " OK, that's another possibility, but I'm sure I read somewhere about some carpets that are made by children working in terrible conditions.

A: Yes, but can you see that logo? It's the GoodWeave logo. It means that the carpet factories have been inspected, so the ones on this website are OK.

B: So, let's just check the prices, though. It sounds like they might cost a fortune. Wow!

A: Yeah … OK, let's try something else … what's this?

B: Oh yeah, silk. Well, that used to be a luxury thing, but is it still so special?

A: What about old silk? That's different. Here's a section on antique silk wall hangings. They're gorgeous.

B: Yeah, that's a good idea, I suppose. If they aren't made anymore, it's unique.

A: OK, so most of these antique textiles were made in Vietnam and Laos, and can't be found anywhere else. It says they've been carefully selected and they only sell pieces that are in excellent condition, despite their age.

A: Well, what do you think? Is there something here we could buy her?

▶ 57
1 This one was hand-made,
2 but these days they are mass-produced.
3 It's been used to put flowers in for the last ten years.
4 It's made of thick blue glass
5 and it contained some kind of medicine originally.

▶ 59
For those of you who enjoy long train trips, we have news of a new route that will soon be completed. Eventually, you'll be able to go by rail all the way from London to the Caspian Sea. Much of this epic railway has already been built across the Caucasus Mountains. The Baku–Tbilisi–Kars railway—or BTK railway—will link the Azerbaijani capital of Baku with Kars, in Turkey. Then a rail tunnel underneath Istanbul will be opened in the next few years, linking East and West in an echo of the trade routes of 1,000 years ago. Both passengers and goods will be carried, and the rail link will transport oil products west and take European goods east.

One of the first east–west trade routes was, of course, the Silk Road, which was made famous to many by the Italian merchant Marco Polo about 700 years ago. Marco Polo's journal tells us many details of the trade that was carried out between China, India, Arabia, and Europe. Luxurious silks, aromatic spices, and precious stones were imported from the East, and cargoes of fine glassware and exotic perfumes were exported from Europe. While goods such as paper, ink, and silk were transported west across the overland routes—the Silk Road—there were other products, such as Chinese ceramics, that had to be transported by sea. These sea-trade routes had been used since long before the time of Marco Polo, and in the centuries after Marco Polo's time they became much more important. Spices in particular—such as black pepper, cinnamon, cardamom, and ginger—were brought from Asia to Europe in what was then known as the Spice Route. and the control of these sea-trade routes was the driving force behind the European exploration which is known as "the Age of Discovery." The Portuguese, Spanish, and British Empires were all based on keeping control of both the routes and the places where spices and other goods were produced. Nowadays, of course, it's oil rather than spices that drives the world economy. And there is no doubt that oil from the Caspian Sea is the main reason why the new rail link across the Caucasus Mountains is being built.

▶ 61
S = salesperson, C = customer
1 S: Can I help you?
   C: No, thanks. I'm just looking.
2 S: Is it for you?
   C: No, it's for my mother.
3 S: Would you like me to gift wrap it?
   C: No thanks, that's OK.
4 S: Do you want to pay by card or in cash?
   C: I'll use my card.
5 S: What time is best for us to deliver it?
   C: In the morning, any day of the week.

Unit 10

▶ 62
W: How was your trip to Canada?
M: It was absolutely stunning, but I wouldn't like to live there.
W: Really? Why is that?
M: I think it would be difficult for me to get used to the cold weather. It was 15 degrees below zero some days! The local people don't seem to notice it so much.
W: If I lived somewhere that cold, I'd never leave the house! Even if I had the warmest, high-tech clothes!
M: Well, they have lots of stuff that makes life a little easier. For example, you can start your car without leaving the house, and this warms up the engine and heats up the inside of the car before you get in.
W: Really? That's a good idea. How does that work?
M: It's just like a remote-control thing—you know, like locking and unlocking the car from a distance.
W: Oh yeah. Well, that would be good if you had to go out when it was really cold. I suppose I would eat a lot in a climate like that, though. I'd put on tons of weight, sitting at home, eating, looking at the snow through the window!
M: You say that, but I'm sure it would be different if you really lived there.
W: Maybe. I'd rather live somewhere hot, though. It's easier to stay cool than to get warm.
M: Do you think so? Do you mean if you had air conditioning in your house?
W: Yes, sort of. But also you could avoid the heat really easily, I think. Get up early when it's cool, have a nap in the middle of the day, that kind of thing.
M: I don't like sleeping in the afternoon very much.
W: OK, but you would have to rest—even if you didn't sleep—if it was over 40 degrees outside.
M: I just couldn't imagine living like that.
W: So really what you're saying is, you're happy where you are?
M: Yes, I suppose so. Aren't I lucky?

▶ 63
1 I'm not sure you would feel that way
2 If I lived somewhere that cold,
3 Well, it would make it warmer
4 You could deal with the hot afternoons

a I'd never go outside.
b if you had a good fire.
c if you took a nap.
d if you really lived there.

▶ 65

H = host, G = guest

H: It's time once again for our "CineScience" feature, where we look at how movies deal with science and how realistically they show scientific ideas. This week our guest is the neurologist, Dr. Clare Law. We're looking at the movie *Limitless,* which came out several years ago, and is now on DVD. The idea of the movie is that we only use 20 percent of our brain power. What would happen if we could use all 100 percent of our brain's potential? Well, in the movie, the main character takes a special pill that lets him do exactly that. And what happens? He writes a book. He learns to speak Italian. He becomes a master of martial arts. So, Clare, does that mean that we could all be like this if we knew how to take advantage of our brains properly?

G: Well, sadly, it's just a movie. And as is often the case in movies, the science is not 100 percent accurate. Of course, it would be unrealistic to think there was a special pill that could unlock our brain power in a flash. But it's not even true that we only use 20 percent of our brain. It's not as simple as that. What actually happens is that we use different parts of the brain at different times and for different functions. So, if you were walking to work, the part of your brain that deals with physical movement would be active. If you were baking a cake, then a different part of your brain would be busy. In other words, there are no unused or hidden regions that are waiting to be discovered and exploited. It would be incredibly inefficient for our bodies to only use 20 percent of the brain. We're using all of our brain all day and we actually already have limitless brain power.

H: So, that's good news. And remember what the character in the movie did with his limitless power. Wrote a book, learned a language and a new skill. It doesn't take a genius to achieve this. These are things that we could all manage to do—if we used our own limitless brain power more efficiently.

G: Exactly.

▶ 67

1 S: I think I was bitten by a mosquito last night.
   R: Why don't you put some of this cream on the bite?
2 S: Look at my finger! I cut it on something. It's bleeding.
   R: You'd better wash it under the tap.
3 S: My ankle is really in pain, and I can't walk.
   R: If I were you, I'd go to the emergency room and get it X-rayed.
4 S: My son has been feeling sick since he ate those oysters.
   R: He might be allergic to them—I'd keep an eye on him.
5 S: I did something to my wrist last week, and it still hurts.
   R: Really? You should get it looked at.

Unit 11

▶ 68

H = host, J = Jo Makeba

H: It's often said that good news never makes the headlines. And it's true that we don't usually hear about wildlife issues unless there's a disaster or a catastrophe somewhere. Then for a day or maybe two, we see front-page headlines and lurid images on our television screens. But there are many success stories. The challenge has always been to tell the rest of the world what's going on. Jo Makeba is going to tell us more.

J: Yes, that's right. I've been looking at how some organizations are using social media to tell their stories. It's so much easier these days for small-scale organizations to have a direct connection with a wide audience.

H: And with people who might be interested in their work?

J: Yes, and also of course, the people who might be able to fund their work. So a good example is the wildlife organization WildlifeDirect.

H: And what exactly is WildlifeDirect?

J: Well, it was started by the Kenyan conservationist Richard Leakey to provide a space online for African conservationists. You could find blogs about gorillas in Virunga National Park, or campaigns to help lions in Kenya. You didn't need to wait for a story to make it into the traditional news media.

H: I remember hearing the story about the gorillas.

J: Exactly. It was WildlifeDirect that told that story to the world. But as social media has changed, so has the approach of WildlifeDirect. You can see this with their campaign "Hands Off Our Elephants," which uses Facebook and Twitter to reach the public. People see stories on social media and it really changes things—in three years, the number of elephants that were killed in Kenya went down by more than eighty percent.

H: That's incredible!

J: Exactly. People reacted to stories by signing petitions or joining public marches and now laws that protect wildlife in Kenya are changing too.

H: On the other hand, I sometimes think that social media has limitations. I mean, you do hear people say "Oh, I'm not on social media anymore" these days.

J: I agree, but I think that's a small minority. However, it's interesting that at the same time as WildlifeDirect uses social media, their Chief Executive Paula Kahumbu also writes regular features in traditional media—in the *Guardian* newspaper. And Paula was also involved in a series of wildlife documentaries, called *NTV Wild,* that started in 2016 on Kenyan TV.

H: It sounds like WildlifeDirect understands how to use 21st-century media very well!

▶ 69

1 You said you knew how to do that.
2 They said it was in the paper.
3 They asked me if I would feed their cat.
4 You said you weren't hungry.
5 You said you could speak Russian.
6 You said you'd cleaned everything up.

▶ 71

How does language change over time? Are there words that we simply stop using? Are there words that we have been using for hundreds or even thousands of years? And how will languages change in this age of global media and social networking? Researchers at the University of Reading, in the United Kingdom, have been investigating exactly these questions.

Biologist Mark Pagel has studied 87 languages from Europe, the Middle East, and the Indian subcontinent that are all related to each other. He took 200 words which he knew had a shared history going back 9,000 years. Words like *who* and *three,* and their equivalents in the 87 different languages. The list of 200 words includes nouns like *salt* and *name,* verbs like *give* and *stand,* and adjectives like *new* and *yellow.* With the help of a computer program, Pagel analyzed all the data relating to these 200 words. The result of the analysis shows that the five oldest words of the 200—in other words, the ones that have not changed very much since ancient times—are *I, two, five, three,* and *who*. These words have hardly changed their sounds and forms. They are also some of the words that we use most in day-to-day speech and so that could be the reason why they have been so stable. The computer analysis, as well as taking a lot less time to look at the data, also highlights patterns that might be difficult to see. For example, it reveals that in all the languages in the study, verbs and adjectives change faster than nouns. Now it's the job of the human analysts to come up with an explanation for this.

▶ 72
1   Can I call you back?
2   Could you call me later?
3   I wonder whether I could leave my name?
4   Can you give me your number?
5   I wonder if you can tell him I called?
6   Could you ask her to call me?

▶ 73
P = patient, R = receptionist
1   P: Can I speak to the doctor, please?
    R: I'm afraid the doctor is with a patient at the moment.
2   P: Oh no. It's about my next appointment.
    R: OK, could you give me your name?
3   P: Yes, it's John Watson. I can't get to my appointment today.
    R: OK, thanks. Can I give you a new appointment time?
4   P: Thanks. Can you make it in the morning, please?
    R: Of course. Can you come on Friday at nine o'clock?
5   P: Yes, that's fine. Thank you.
    R: Thank you for calling. Bye.

Unit 12

▶ 74
1
W: Nice to see you back. Are you feeling better now?
M: Yes, a lot better actually since I finally finished taking those tablets.
W: What were they? Antibiotics?
M: Yeah. I can't imagine what we would do without antibiotics. And apparently it was just by chance that they were discovered.
W: I know. But I think that even if Fleming hadn't discovered them—or penicillin, anyway—some other scientist would have eventually.
M: Yes, I suppose so. There was so much medical research going on in those days.
W: And today, as well.

2
A: I wonder how serious the issue of deforestation in rural Kenya would have become if it hadn't been for the Green Belt Movement?
B: You mean the Green Belt Movement that was created by the activist, Wandari Maathai?
A: Yes. She spoke about how each individual in a community needed to work together to make a difference, and many women were motivated to help reduce deforestation.
B: Do you know how successful the movement has been?
A: Well, since 1977, over 51 million trees have been planted, and over 30,000 women have been trained in various trades.

B: That's amazing.
A: Yes, it is. Did you know that Wandari Maathai won a Nobel Prize in 2004 for her work?
3
D= Dad, P = Paul
D: I can't find that website you told me about, Paul.
P: Have you typed it in correctly? Let's see. Look, you left part out.
D: What?
P: The forward slashes after "http." Actually, I read that Tim Berners-Lee said he could have left them out.
D: Well, it would have been a lot easier if he had! I wouldn't have wasted so much time typing.
P: Actually Dad, it's easier if you copy and paste the address in.
D: Well, I could have done that if the address had been on the screen somewhere! But you told me it on the phone.
P: Or you could have used Google …
D: Oh, yes. I suppose so. I hadn't thought of Google.

4
A: Did you see the movie they made about Dian Fossey?
B: Yes, I thought it was pretty good. It makes you wonder what might have happened if she'd lived.
A: But why was she murdered, really?
B: It was never investigated well. She might have upset the local poachers too many times.
A: But she'd always had problems with them—or at least that's what it said in the movie.
B: Exactly. Or it might have been because she'd had a lot of trouble with the authorities. She was against that kind of wildlife tourism that goes into remote areas.
A: Well, one thing's for sure, the gorillas would be better protected if she were still alive.

▶ 75
1   Captain Scott led two expeditions to Antarctica.
2   On the second, they were racing another team to the South Pole.
3   This picture shows team members preparing a sled.
4   Some people say they might have been the first to the South Pole. . .
5   . . . if they hadn't used this type of transportation.
6   And they might not have died on the return journey.

▶ 77
I suppose that in one way, we could say that all animals have to be experts at what they do. If they weren't, well, they wouldn't survive. The truth is that the day-to-day life of most animals is about finding something to eat while trying not to become food for another animal. So we could say that, for example, the polar bear or the lion is an expert hunter. Or the chameleon is an expert at camouflage. But some animals seem to us to be particularly skilled. These are the ones that seem to be able to take their expertise to a different level, especially in a laboratory or a controlled study environment.

Let's take the octopus as an example. These marine animals can do extraordinary things in their natural habitat. The common octopus can almost instantaneously mimic the colors, patterns, and even textures of its surroundings. Predators swim by without even noticing it. And if a predator does notice it, the octopus squirts a cloud of black ink at the predator, which gives it just enough time to get quickly away.

But we can see how clever the octopus really is when we take it out of its natural environment and bring it into the laboratory. Put a nice tasty food item like a shrimp in a closed jar, and then put the jar in a tank. Next, put an octopus in the tank as well. It will actually take the lid off the jar to get at the shrimp! So not only does the octopus work out how to get into the jar, it also has the physical ability to do it. And that's not all. At a laboratory in Seattle, in the United States, a giant Pacific octopus was actually getting out of its tank at night, going to the other tanks, eating the fish in them, and then going back to its own tank. It was only the trail of water on the floor that gave the laboratory staff a clue to what was going on!

▶ 79

1 S: You forgot to text me!
   R: Oh, yes. Sorry about that!
2 S: I'm so sorry. I didn't have time to cook anything special.
   R: There's no need to apologize. It's not a problem.
3 S: This door is open!
   R: It's my fault. I forgot to lock it.
4 S: I'm sorry, but I think I lost the magazine you lent me.
   R: Don't worry about it. I'd already read it.
5 S: I can't believe I forgot about that! I'm really sorry.
   R: It's not your fault. It could have happened to anyone.